She Speaks

Breaking the Silence of Shame

D1411747

Kate Troyer

Dedication

This book is dedicated to my Mom

God handpicked you to be my mom because He knew I'd need a strong mother to impart to me the ability to become a warrior. Though some of our years were difficult, and we didn't understand each other, it is because of you that I breathe fire today. Your courage in the face of adversity, in many painful life moments, showed me the example of what it means when the fire within burns brighter than the fire which sought to consume me. For never giving up on life, for never surrendering to that which sought to kill your spirit, I honor you.

Acknowledgments

With special thanks to:

My parents for being students of life. The culture we came from didn't put a lot of stock in scholastics, but you both were avid students of this adventure called life. In whatever state you found yourselves in, you both sought to make the best of a situation by looking for the silver lining. You took what you were taught and added what you observed in other people's lives to be expedient. I'm grateful for both of your heart's desires to never stop learning. You are both young at heart.

Mom, your courage and resilience taught me to be the strong woman I am today. I'm forever grateful that God gave me you for my Mom. I love you!

Dad, for showing me how to talk to God as a friend and for being my biggest fan. I love you!

Tresa Davis, for listening and agreeing with me that my voice shall be heard even if only the dishes I'm washing hears it. From tiny voice to bigger voice, what you do matters more than you know.

Charity Bradshaw, my coach and mentor, for your faith in me and for shining light into the darkest moments of this journey as I faced the girl in the mirror and finally said what she wished to say when her mouth was still covered.

Ivan, the steady, immovable rock in my world. After twenty-two years of practicing marriage, you're still the best man I know.

Kara, for all the ways you're not like me and for the ways you are, I love you and couldn't be more proud to be your mom. I admire your strength, compassion, and gracious spirit. "Let her sleep for when she wakes she moves mountains."

Ty, I admire the way you seek to be the voice for those who don't have one. I respect your passion for justice. In your lifetime, you will move mountains. I love you and am ever so proud to have you for my son.

My siblings:

Marvin, for being a man who speaks in parables and who values the strength of a woman and encourages her to become the author of her life more than any man I know.

Susie, for being the wind beneath my wings from childhood and for being a warrior for justice.

Emma, for your quiet strength that brings peace to others and your support of me through all of it.

Hannah, for your can-do attitude and your exuberant optimism that splashes on those around you.

Dean, for your no-nonsense view of life and the inspiration to be true to one's beliefs regardless of what others think.

Dorothy, for your optimism and expressions of loving support of those closest to you.

Joanna, for being the butterfly in my life and for being the one who in every situation makes life better by filling it with splashes of light.

Gina, for bringing laughter to every family gathering and for being a champion for the underdog.

And finally:

Courtney Artiste, for your gracious response to all my questions, concerns, and fears. For the work you do, Thank you!

Table of Contents

Dedication

Acknowledgements

1   Introduction

3   Chapter 1: Fear Beyond My Years

11   Chapter 2: Blanket of Shame

15   Chapter 3: Lie Hide Protect

19   Chapter 4: Rite of Passage

25   Chapter 5: The Girl in the Mirror

29   Chapter 6: Flawed

35   Chapter 7: Arrested Development

39   Chapter 8: New Beginnings

43   Chapter 9: Love and Heartbreak

47   Chapter 10: Courtship and the Wedding

53   Chapter 11: Reset

57   Chapter 12: Transition and Motherhood

63   Chapter 13: Lost Found and Angel Babies

71   Chapter 14: Redemption

77   Chapter 15: Finding My Footing

83   Chapter 16: Walls Crumbling

95   Chapter 17: Light Filled Cracks

97   Chapter 18: Fear Lies and Truth

107 Chapter 19: Caterpillar to Butterfly

115 Chapter 20: No is A Good Word

123 Chapter 21: Unlovable

129 Chapter 22: Beautiful

135 Chapter 23: Credit or No Credit

141 Chapter 24: A Place of Grace

149 Chapter 25: Blessing My Body

153   Chapter 26: A Place of Peace

157   Chapter 27: Broken Gifts

163   Chapter 28: Beautifully Imperfect

171   Chapter 29: Lies Appearing True

175   Chapter 30: Authentically Me

        About the Author

        Contact Information

Introduction

This book is about the experience and perspective of me, the author. The older I get, the more I realize that so many experiences in life are seen through the lenses we look through now. It may well be that just as my perspective changed from youth to adulthood, in a year from now, I may not see things the same as I do today. My goal in life is to never stop growing, always seeking to learn, adapt and grow, all the while being grounded and content in whatever state I may find myself. That being said, may I never lose my sense of wonder.

Fear Beyond My Years

What if I was given this journey to walk so that I may understand, overcome, and heal because He knew I would be strong enough? That in my healing and restoration, others might be healed also. ~ Kate Troyer

I came into this world kicking and screaming with the umbilical cord wrapped around my neck twice. Due to complications, the midwife told my mom she hadn't expected me to be born alive. I was alive, and that's when the crying began. For the better part of the first year of my life, when at weddings or at church, ladies would come running with mashed potatoes, or applesauce, noodles, or soup, to quiet this wee one whose wails pierced the cheerful hum of conversation usually heard in these events. Alas, I wouldn't be still.

Doctor said it was just colic, and I'd grow out of it.

I have heard this story relayed numerous times over the years. What was wrong with me? Yes, the doctors that my mom went to for help decided that it was just colic and that I'd grow out of it, but why did I cry without ceasing unless I was in pain?

I felt sad for the little one who suffered for lack of knowing what was wrong and guilty for the stress my parents endured with this supposed to be beautiful baby girl who proved anything but happy and delightful in her first year.

*   *   *   *   *

And so I grew in height and personality. After the crying ceased, I was a quiet, peaceable girl who loved to play with dolls and on the playground. Eager to please those around me, I played well with siblings and friends.

One of my favorite and earliest memories involves helping my dad do chores on our dairy farm. I helped him throw big piles of straw from the second floor of the barn downstairs to the main floor for bedding for the cows, at least as well as a four-year-old could help. I loved watching the straw rush down the opening of the barn floor and then a few individual pieces as they floated slowly to the cement floor at the bottom. But then …

*   *   *   *   *

Suddenly, I awoke in a loud, bright room with strange people milling about. A tall man with a booming voice said, "Hey, you're sucking on your finger?" I turned my face toward the wall to hide. I really wanted to stop using my index finger as a pacifier, but that was much easier said than done. I had no idea where I was. Oddly enough, I wasn't scared. Soon my dad's face came into view with a nurse following him to escort me in a small crib to a private room where I'd stay until observation of my concussion was completed. Dad bought me a gray stuffed donkey that was nearly as big as I was to keep me company. A man with a white coat, big floppy shoes, and a funny, big, red nose stopped to make me laugh. After three days, it was time for me to return home to my mom and siblings, one who was only a few months old.

*   *   *   *   *

When I returned home, Mom explained to me that I went down with a pile of straw, landing on bare cement eight feet below. The hired hand found me and hurriedly carried me to my mom in the front yard where she held me waiting for the ambulance. The closest phone was a half a mile away, which my dad raced to on his bike. He drove with one hand as one arm was in a sling due to him breaking it a few days before.

I recovered quickly and never felt pain beyond a slight, dull headache.

*   *   *   *   *

I worried about things that should've been years beyond my comprehension. For instance, in first grade, my teacher who shared my first name, gave me a most beautiful doll in the school Christmas gift exchange. I had my best friend Ana's name. Mom helped me choose a great gift, or so I thought, until my friend stated that she wanted a doll too. I couldn't enjoy my doll for weeks due to Ana's disappointment in what Mom deemed a perfectly acceptable gift.

I worried about safety from thunderstorms, afraid lightning would strike me or a bad man would steal me when my parents weren't watching closely enough.

As far back as I can remember, I experienced debilitating anxiety. I recall that on numerous occasions, my mom would put ointment on my chest to lessen the intense, literal heart pain I felt. I now know the pain was caused by anxiety. My parents could be in the same room sitting next to me, but I refused to be comforted. In some instances, life events supported the anxiety.

*   *   *   *   *

At age seven, two of my sister's and I were sitting in our family's jet black buggy that we used for transportation back in the day with Bobby. Bobby was our retired, but spirited, sixteen-year-old, black as night with a white star on his forehead, racehorse. He was harnessed and waiting to take us to a friend's house for dinner as I sat on the seat dreaming of a fun evening with my friend Annie.

Suddenly, the buggy lurched forward as the horse discovered the rope that had tied him to the grape arbor post in the front yard had come undone. I yanked my two-year-old sister, who'd been standing on the step outside the buggy balancing herself by looping her hand through the velvet strap attached to the inside of it, on to the seat beside me.

I looked back to see my mom fall to her knees in the front yard praying the horse would be stopped. As the horse raced out the gravel lined driveway, with mere seconds to react, I grabbed for the frayed, braided reigns, but only one remained inside the buggy. I grasped it with both hands and pulled with all my might. The horse responded with a quick side step, pulling us into the shallow ditch right next to the barnyard fence. He pranced, jerking on the reign, wanting desperately to continue the sprint he'd started.

Just as he began to pull us back onto the driveway, my dad came into view, talking to Bobby, coaxing him to calm down and halt. My young heart was never more relieved. We returned to the barnyard to gather the rest of the family and were soon on our way. Fear paralyzed my tongue, and as was my habit, I hid it away in my heart. I couldn't talk about the incident for quite some time.

As I did with every other scary or uncomfortable event, I bottled the emotions up and stored them in my heart as anxiety and nausea over the tension I carried in my stomach grew ever stronger.

*   *   *   *   *

No amount of anxiety can change the future. No amount of regret can change the past. ~ Karen Salmansohn

Fear Beyond My Years

Blanket of Shame

Shame is a soul eating emotion. ~ C. G. Jung

As fast as my little legs could carry me, I ran toward the open door of the rusty, blue van, grasped the armrest by the indented handle, and practically vaulted inside. I climbed onto the seat next to my sisters and scooted back. With proper aplomb, I adjusted my olive-green dress, hugged my favorite doll tightly to myself, and readied for the twenty-minute drive to my Aunt Sandy's house. The gravel crunched loudly as we pulled into the driveway. Barely parked, we rushed out to play with cousins for the day. The aroma of barbecue chicken baking greeted us as we walked through the door. Aunt Sandy greeted us with slices of fresh baked, crusty bread slathered with shaken in a jar until formed, homemade butter. After finishing every morsel of chicken and bread, we hurried off to play with barbeque stained mouths.

Hours passed with imaginary trips to the store for food and diapers for our "babies," complete with doctor's appointments for one very sick baby and another who needed a check-up. Older cousin Seth came into the room and asked me to be his patient at the doctor's office. I followed him to the space between the wall and the twin sized bed in my aunt's guest bedroom. At five-years-old, I didn't know to like or dislike this. I didn't look at him as he played doctor, but I was happy when he said I could go play again. Soon after, we were told that it was time to go home.

* * * * *

Back at home, my parents gathered my siblings and I in the living room and sat us down to talk. Confused, I listened as Mom told of how Aunt Sandy saw what I let Seth do to me and that is was a terrible, shameful thing.

While my siblings watched and waited with somber expressions, it was decided I was to be taken to the bedroom and spanked. There were only a few of my siblings there, but when I revisited this painful place in my early thirties, it felt as though a hundred accusers surrounded my living room as I received my reprimand, watching and agreeing with the accusation that the little five-year-old me was tarnished goods.

Today, I realize that my mom felt scared and panicked and decided to make an example of me in hopes that no such thing would happen to me or my siblings again, but in my innocence, I took responsibility for what was done to me. I accepted a blanket of guilt and shame that I carried into my thirties.

* * * * *

Like a tidal wave crashing over me, rushing in to meet me here. Your love is fierce. ~ Jesus Culture

Blanket of Shame

3

Lie Hide Protect

We cannot forever hide the truth about ourselves, from ourselves.
~ John McCain

What if I were to admit that I've been less than honest most of my life? It started out with me cringing in fear in reaction to Mom's stern voice when she discovered a discarded household item that I wasn't allowed to play with on the floor. I'd quickly respond, "Wasn't me!" when it was in fact me. Then I'd get in trouble for lying. It would've turned out better for me many times over if I'd simply said, "It was me, Mom."

On one such occasion, I heard Mom ask who had been playing with the turkey baster she kept in the utensil drawer in the kitchen.

I was quick to answer, "Not me!" Mom said she saw me play with it, and since I lied, I had to wait until Dad got home from work to receive my punishment.

The day dragged on forever. After a painful day of waiting for the dreaded spanking, I decided to go to bed, hoping Mom and Dad would forget about my promised punishment.

No such luck. Dad came home, heard of my wrongdoing, and suggested that maybe it'd be better to just get the punishment over with. Afterwards, I was greatly relieved to know that there was no need to dread the next day.

*   *   *   *   *

When I was about six, the whole family was playing outside, and each of us got a piece of candy. Mom put the candy in the little yellow block spring house at the end of the sidewalk which housed the milk from the dairy cows until the milkman arrived to haul it to the cheese house for cheese making. We were instructed to leave the candy be.

My sister, who was just younger than me, was spotted with another piece of candy. Mom asked who gave it to her, but no one answered. It was decided that I had to have given it to her since my sister couldn't have reached it. I emphatically stated that I didn't touch it, but I got spanked anyway. I felt betrayed. My little mind decided that the truth didn't count. I realize now that since I had a habit of lying, it was good cause to believe that this time was no different, but to my young heart, it was an incredibly painful moment.

*   *   *   *   *

While riding the bus to school one day at age eleven, we stopped to pick up my best friend Mary. Like every other morning, I scooted over to make room for her to sit with me. She leaned in to whisper to me that her mom was pregnant again. I stated that I knew. When she asked how I knew, I explained that I heard a friend of my mom's talk about it. I wasn't supposed to know about it since pregnancy wasn't discussed openly.

When I got home, my mom said she had gotten a call from Mary's mom and asked me why I told Mary that I knew her mom was pregnant. I said I didn't tell her. Lie. Hide. Protect. Thus, began phone conversations and a meeting between the parents. My parents defending me and Mary's parents defending her. I decided I was in this far, so I couldn't admit guilt now.

The incident gradually faded from everyone else's memory, but it stayed at the forefront of my mind. I felt happiness-stealing guilt for more than two years, until one morning, I couldn't handle the guilt a moment longer. I approached my dad after finishing morning chores and asked him to pray with me. I confessed the lie, and he suggested I call Mary's mom and apologize. I felt incredibly light and happy.

*　　*　　*　　*　　*

Always speak the truth, even if your voice shakes.
~ Anonymous

Rite of Passage

Wherever you go, go with all your heart. ~ Confucius

I'd begun to blossom into a woman at the age of eleven. I was pleased to be maturing and looked forward to wearing a dress that closed in the front, complete with a pinned cape that crossed over my developing bosom and an apron with a belt that looped around my waist instead of dresses that buttoned down the back. It also meant I'd be able to sit with the older girls at church.

The first day of this rite of passage dawned bright and sunny, the first Sunday after my twelfth birthday. With morning chores and breakfast done, we hurried to set everything just right, since church was to be held at our home on this Sunday.

19

The hay loft was emptied, swept clean, and set up with wooden, backless benches lined in long rows. Soon everyone arrived, and it was time for services to begin. In my new, freshly ironed dress of royal blue, I followed the girls to the back row of the women's section and sat with my back perfectly straight. I wouldn't slouch on this momentous occasion.

The married men and young single men sat across from us. It was the perfect way to sneak a glance at the cute young men in their Sunday best. Although this one didn't do much glancing since it was too difficult to make eye contact without blushing profusely, the bane of my young existence. Not only did I know I was painfully shy with a beet red face, but others did too.

The three-hour service finally ended with a song sang with gusto as everyone eagerly anticipated lunch. After devouring chicken and noodles, fresh homemade bread, Amish peanut butter spread, pickles, pickled red beets, and cheese, we ended the meal with a variety of cookies that all the church ladies brought along with coffee and tea.

Relaxing after the noon meal, one of those cute, young men commented that I looked angry during service. I insisted I wasn't mad as I blushed and purposed in my heart that I must learn to smile. The desire to remain a wallflower grew.

The day ended with dinner for the youth group and a time of singing. Then the young men with girlfriends would go to her house for a few hours to spend their weekly date on her living room sofa to discuss matters of mutual interest. No doubt, they were planning for their future together, as was customary in the community I grew up in.

* * * * *

Monday came, and life went on as usual. Mom had explained a few weeks earlier that I may soon start what was called a period. I felt disgusted with the subject and wanted nothing to do with it. To my understanding, my body was to serve me, but I had not a clue about its preassigned purpose. I was intrigued by femininity, but I did my best to ignore this body of mine. I did not want to talk about that embarrassing subject. I just wanted to continue life without any more changes.

Waking up one morning to find the telltale sign of "that," I hurried to the bathroom, found a maxi pad, and cried for innocence lost. I felt betrayed by my body. I thought to myself, "I'll never be normal again." As was my habit, I washed my face, shut off my emotions, and faced the day.

As my body changed, my anxiety grew. I crawled further into my shell. I felt so insecure. I rarely talked to anyone outside of family and a few close friends. I was still frequently asked why I was mad. I made the decision to start smiling, so people quit asking why I was mad. Smiling became my way of dealing with the world in its entirety.

As my anxiety grew, I discovered that if I ate until it hurt, I didn't feel as anxious. Where my stomach had hurt due to anxiety, it now hurt from too much food. The anxiety peaked at night. My subconscious knew that bad things happened at night. I feared the night because it wasn't safe to me, and I hated it. Filling my body with more food seemed to be the method of choice to deal with it.

*   *   *   *   *

Until you heal the wounds of your past, you are going to bleed. You can bandage the bleeding with food, with alcohol, with drugs, with work, with cigarettes, with sex; But eventually, it will all ooze through and stain your life. You must find the strength to open the wounds, stick your hands inside, pull out the core of the pain that is holding you in your past, the memories and make peace with them. ~ Iyanla Vanzant

Rite of Passage

5

The Girl in the Mirror

Talk to yourself like you would to someone you love.
~ Brene Brown

For an Amish girl, a tiny waist is essential to be "ideal," and ideal disappeared as my body developed.

One morning, as I put on my best dress for church, Mom was helping me pin the pleats on the back of my cape in place. She commented that I was getting chunky. I didn't know much about chunky, but I knew enough to know it wasn't a good thing.

On the outside, my facial expression remained unchanged, but inside, my heart plummeted as these words stirred the deeply embedded belief that I was indeed flawed. I had never heard the term chunky to describe me since I'd always been skinny. Newly aware of my chunky self, I grew ever more awkward.

In my room, while getting ready for school, I'd stand before the mirror looking at the young, scared image who kept changing and stared back at me with utter disdain. I didn't know her anymore. I avoided eye contact with her, but as I looked at her body, I mocked the defeated, ugly, fat person I saw.

Shortly after this, one day after school, Mom saw me eating a cookie and said, "Katie, you really shouldn't eat that." Angry inside, I tiptoed into the pantry, polished off two cookies, and waltzed back into the kitchen as if nothing happened. Thus, began my habit of eating in secret. Even if it would've occurred to me that I'd wear what I ate in secret, I don't think it would've made a difference because I needed the food to protect my ever-growing anxiety over the things I couldn't control.

Today I realize that what Mom said was out of love and concern for my future, an attempt to help me and wanting the very best for her daughter, and I receive it as such. But at the time, it was another area where I was flawed, less than enough, and alone. I wanted so very desperately to be accepted for me, for who I was and not criticized for who I wasn't. Alone, I wrestled with the demons of the night. Loneliness drove me to seek God. I called, but He didn't answer, or at least to my understanding He didn't. My cry at night, when I was alone, was that I just wanted to be heard.

*   *   *   *   *

With every opportunity I had, I'd announce to my friends that I was fat. Today, I know that it's a terrible feeling to hear someone harm their beautiful body with words, but I wanted my friends to know that I knew I was flawed before they had a chance to think of it on their own, which I felt sure would only be a matter of time. My sweet friends showed more patience with me than was fair regarding my self-image and frequently assured me that I wasn't fat. I knew they were just being nice. There was no doubt, I was indeed fat!

I spent years thinking that if I could just reach my goal weight, my life would be perfect.

Isn't it funny that when one detail grows to gigantic proportion, it drowns out any other thing? The truth is that there were many lies I believed, and excess weight was one side effect of my choice of coping. Because the extra weight was glaringly obvious, it didn't occur to me that had I lost the extra weight, some other detail would've grown to giant status.

* * * * *

A little more kindness, a little less judgment.

Flawed

Shame says that because I'm flawed I am unacceptable. Grace says that though I am flawed I am cherished.
~ Michelle Graham

In ways we don't realize, there are times that we as human beings help accusations carry more weight than is our intention.

For me, it was the look of pity I received from people close to me. A look that said, "I feel terrible that you are flawed like this. I can't imagine how you do it. You can't possibly be happy." These looks affected me deeply.

When an acquaintance said to me, "You have such a pretty face...," followed by the look, "It's just unfortunate that your body doesn't match," it left me reeling, seeking solid footing.

In trying to crawl out of the pit I continually found myself in, it was these looks and comments that strengthened the accusations of the flawed individual I saw myself as.

In seeking to refute the lies, I heard, "See, even they think you're flawed." I'm convinced that even well-meaning people who were close to me, those who made my life more difficult in moments, were a gift to me. Had a stranger given me those looks, I may have been hurt or angry, but I would've walked away and that would've been the end of it, but when the hard things came from those close to me, I couldn't run from it. I had to sit with the discomfort, but every such experience has had a blessing in it for me.

In zeroing in on the extra weight I carried, it shut out any other good qualities I could've focused on. Thus, I became one big disappointment, with the support of others agreeing with me and strengthening my belief that I was flawed.

*　*　*　*　*

One of the ways that being overweight was a gift to me was that I was a quiet, well-behaved young girl. I was too scared of God to willfully do wrong, so my parents lucked out in that way. Since I couldn't be the weight I thought was acceptable to others, not speaking was a way that I could be invisible.

I couldn't attain the societal ideal of weighing a proper weight, therefore, I had to dig in and find me worth fighting for from within because I realized it wasn't going to come from without.

If I could share one piece of advice, it would be to never again feel sorry for someone who's overweight. Pity does not assist or encourage a person. Instead, it hurts them.

People who shop or gamble to cope with their problems appear to be normal people on the surface, but an overweight person's way of coping is visible, so they appear more flawed, when in reality, they are no more flawed than anyone else.

In saying this, I don't for a single moment want to give the impression that I'm an advocate for obesity. I'm a strong proponent of a healthy body weight.

I've spent more than twenty years studying health, eating plans, and all things diet related. I know too much to be overweight, but I think this clearly shows that it isn't in what I know as much as it is in what I do.

Knowing all that I know proved to add condemnation for my failures over the years, but today, I'm profoundly grateful for the gift of peace right where I am. For when I tasted of His Divine Love, it flowed into the broken pieces of my heart and mended them eternally.

* * * * *

It's been said that beauty is in the eye of the beholder. When has it ever been more so than today that a certain size and type of body is seen as the perfect example of beauty?

I will never cease to lean into a healthy body weight and the best size for me, however, how square is the box we try to put ourselves into when we try to fit into everyone's definition of perfect?

What if we would begin to fall in love with our bodies, whether curvy or slender, right where we are at this moment?

What if we'd begin anew by embracing who we are right here, right now?

Hating and mistreating my body has served me nothing but heartache. The lie of the pain of not fitting in and worrying about what someone else thought I was supposed to be robbed me of too many peace filled moments.

*   *   *   *   *

Peace. It does not mean to be in a place where there is no noise, trouble, or hard work, it means to be in the midst of those things and still be calm in your heart.
~ Unknown

Flawed

Arrested Development

Success is a journey, not a destination. The doing is often more important than the outcome. ~ Arthur Ashe

I promised myself many times that I wasn't going to write my story until I reached my goal weight. This promise served me well for a number of years. I didn't have to face some of the deepest, darkest parts of my heart as long as I didn't attempt to put them on paper.

When I was thirteen, the statement, "That Katie is so lazy!" made by my mom's maid carried to my ears from around the corner where I stood waiting for church services to start. Again, words had the power to wound, and they found their mark. It became a personal truth. Never mind the fact that at thirteen, a young girl wishes to spend ample time in her room contemplating life and seeking to find her bearings. For me, it was the love of reading. I would prop the stairs door open, race quietly up to my room, and bury my nose in the latest book I was reading. I would keep one ear open so when my mother called from downstairs, I could quickly run to her side, answering with a breathless yes. Today, I understand that the maid, being only a few years older than me, had no patience for my interest in development and was frustrated by my lack of initiative.

At thirteen, I didn't understand this fact. I simply bought into the maid's statement that I was lazy and made it a part of my identity.

*   *   *   *   *

During grade school, I thrived in reading, spelling, and English. Math was altogether a torment for me. I couldn't seem to grasp its concepts. The more math problems the class solved together, the better my grade turned out. From fourth grade on, I flunked math, but since I did well in every other subject, I was promoted to the next grade. This was before special tutoring was available if needed, so it fell into line with my belief that I just wasn't enough.

We received a grade for effort. I'd be devastated when I got a lower grade for effort on my report card. I didn't know how to express my inability to understand math, and the red marks on my report card supported my truth that something was wrong with me. I felt anxiety each quarter when report cards were sent home, and the quiet disappointment I felt from my parents was punishing.

When I graduated eighth grade, I was in my mind, a lazy, overweight, terrible in math student, whose only redeeming quality was that I had a nice personality.

*   *   *   *   *

Perfectionism is not a quest for the best. It is the pursuit of the worst in ourselves, the part that tells us that nothing we do will ever be good enough – that we should try harder. ~ Julia Cameron

Arrested Development

8

New Beginnings

*Authenticity is the daily practice of letting go of who we think
we're supposed to be and embracing who we are.*
~ Brene Brown

At age fourteen, my parents took us to a revival meeting held at the local fire hall in our community, which was strictly prohibited by our church. My heart was pounding as I listened to the preacher talk about eternal salvation. I really wanted to go forward to be prayed for, but I stayed glued to my seat instead. Over the next few days, my parents had many conversations, and I knew that there was change in the air. We attended church a few more times, but we also began to visit a new church.

On a crisp, clean Pennsylvania morning, we headed off to our home church in the horse drawn two-seated buggy. I walked into the house where church was to be held that day and found a corner to stand to wait for services to start. It became clear that my friends knew that something was amiss when not one of them talked to me before or after services. Clearly, everyone had been warned to stay away from me because our family had a new and strange belief. I left that day with a touch of rejection and sadness, but having heard personal accounts of how one could have a personal relationship with God, I felt a peaceful resolve that my life as an Amish girl had come to an end. The next Sunday we visited the new church again and never looked back.

*   *   *   *   *

The day after Christmas, a few weeks later, as I finished my morning chores, guilt weighed heavy for lies I'd told that affected others. I asked my dad to pray with me. I asked Jesus to be Lord of my life, confessed my lies, and the weight of the world lifted off my shoulders. Life seemed suddenly brighter and happier.

The next Sunday, as I sat in the new church listening to the preacher's message, I felt at peace and gobbled up the words he shared and was amazed at the things I was hearing. The new church people were friendly and hospitable. That is where I met my lifelong, one who experiences similar things simultaneously or separately, understands that life happens, sometimes we don't talk for months, but we pick up right where we left off the next time we see each other, friend. I thought she was a beautiful girl with lovely straight, medium brown hair. I took note because mine was wavy and a bit unruly.

Miriam and I became fast friends. If I shared anything with anyone, it was Miriam. Albeit very little was said in the way of pouring out our hearts, we spent countless hours together chatting about anything and everything that is of interest to teenage girls, and my heart felt safe with her.

*   *   *   *   *

Friends are medicine for a wounded heart and vitamins for a hopeful soul. ~ Steve Maraboli

41

New Beginnings

Love and Heartbreak

New beginnings are often disguised as painful endings.

When I was around fifteen and still wearing my Amish clothes, I visited a new church and met a young man who left a lasting impression on me. He was handsome and outgoing, and I was immediately smitten. I knew little about him, but I fell in love. Head over heels, heart racing, life altering love. Isn't fifteen too young to fall in love? Apparently not.

I began to dream of a future with him. Distance kept our contact to a minimum, but that didn't keep my heart from wanting him and only him.

I talked to my dad about how I felt. I could sense that Dad didn't approve of my desire. He asked me to put it on a shelf until I got older.

Sixteen arrived with the announcement that the love of my life was dating a beautiful young girl. To say that my heart was broken seems too simple a term to describe what I felt. I couldn't cry. I couldn't eat. I couldn't sleep. I just numbly and methodically carried on with daily responsibilities. My life was over. Happiness was as fleeting as vibrant, autumn leaves.

What is the purpose of falling in love just to have that love disappear from grasp? I sought to know what good purpose, if any, this heartbreak served me. I never did find out why, but I do know that I wouldn't trade my life today for what might have been.

*   *   *   *   *

Over the next few years, in what felt to me like a cult atmosphere church, I continuously heard the importance of seeking out the demons hiding around each corner and ridding myself of them, and fear, shame, and anxiety grew to a feverish pitch. To aspire to holiness, I needed to look into my heart and confess everything I could find in there so that I could approach the throne of God. With fear and trembling, I'd seek every last bad thought, idea, and misdeed and confess them and ask to be prayed for.

Desperate to please God, I inhaled everything the preachers talked about, eagerly confessing every sin I could find in the farthest recesses of my heart. Looking back, I realize that since I was being taught to look into my heart continually, I would always find things to be condemned for. While I found moments of peace by sweeping my heart clean at the latest revival meeting, I couldn't come to a place of abiding peace.

I remember one minister got frustrated because I couldn't understand that I was clean. He insisted that I was clean, but my heart knew there was something missing, something they couldn't give me, but I didn't know how to find that something.

I was convinced that the head minister of our group of churches could read my mind and see if there were any demons hiding in me.

At every revival meeting, I'd respond to the preacher's call to come forward to be prayed for and confess. I confessed past confessed sins, sins I didn't commit, and sins I'd barely thought of committing.

My life became pure torment. Bouncing back and forth between thinking maybe I was alright with God to sinking into utter despair to realize that I was such a failure and could never measure up to this God who stood ready to strike me down if I misstepped.

It was in this time that my husband Ivan and I got married. We had been visiting other churches shortly before our wedding and after. We visited the church where I encountered the God of love and received the all-encompassing love that began to heal my heart. I began to understand that God wasn't angry with me. He in fact loved me and sought a relationship with me.

* * * * *

Love is not only something you feel, it is something you do.
~ David Wilkerson

Courtship and the Wedding

Let go, my soul, & trust in Him the waves and wind still know His name. ~ Kristine DiMarco/Bethel Music

D ad had explained to me a few years before I turned eighteen that he would support me dating once I reached eighteen. I had no problem accepting that, and for some reason, I thought it good counsel. I'm thankful today for his guidance in that area.

With my eighteenth birthday fast approaching, he came to me and said a young man asked to court me and that he'd tell me who it was in the next few weeks. I asked him if it was Ivan, and if so, I wasn't interested. He encouraged me to wait and seek God about it, but instinct told me it was Ivan.

Over the next few weeks, I mulled over my impending "coming of age" birthday. The morning after eighteen arrived, Dad confirmed that Ivan had called him to ask for permission to court me. I clearly understood that this wasn't a "casual date this man to see if I like him decision." It was a "whether to marry this man decision." I asked for a week to think it over. Nervous that I'd have to see him before I gave my answer, I left town to spend the weekend with my friend, Miriam, whose family had recently moved to another city four hours away.

*　*　*　*　*

In considering marriage to Ivan, the facts were that he was my dad's hired hand for many years, our families had known each other since childhood, he was eleven and a half years older than me, and he was a good man. Truth is, I did not ask myself if I loved this man, I just knew that my parents liked and accepted him as a great guy for me.

The church also endorsed our potential union. One member commented that they couldn't wait until Ivan asked to court me, which frustrated me greatly since I was fiercely private and disliked others knowing about my potential life decisions before I did.

I believed that these reasons must mean that it was God's will that I marry Ivan. I knew in my heart that I'd say yes to him, but I wanted a little time before I answered.

When I returned home, I told my dad it was okay for Ivan to call me.

*   *   *   *   *

Our first date was a simple, peaceful day spent walking in the beautiful park at a nearby lake discussing the thoughts each of us had about our future. It ended with a delicious dinner of seafood, where my love affair with shrimp scampi officially began and where Ivan expressed his desire to treat me as a queen. What a sweet man he was!

At the end of our second date, Ivan asked if I wanted to get married. I replied, "yes," and the wedding planning commenced.

Over the next seven months, I began to open my heart to this good man. To remain pure, we were instructed by church leaders that that meant no physical contact, no holding hands or kissing. It was of great importance to me that we stayed pure, for I believed God would punish me dramatically if I were to do anything not deemed acceptable by those in authority in my church.

* * * * *

My wedding day arrived on a chilly, November morning. In the blur that followed, three hundred guests, all dressed in their finest, filled each pew in the sanctuary.

Aware that all eyes were on me as the wedding march began, I found it ever so difficult to meet my guests with an open smile, much less individual eye contact. I could only hope that my face wouldn't choose this moment to turn a bright crimson.

As I walked to the front of the church with my mom on one side and my dad on the other, I looked shyly into my groom's eyes as he smiled lovingly. My dad put my hand in his, wishing us both a happy life together.

After a lengthy ceremony with the odd child protesting over having to sit still for so long, and my pastor finished sharing about the merits of a good marriage, I exchanged vows with this good man, promising to love and cherish him until death us do part. And suddenly, as the pianist played an energetic rendition of Joyful, Joyful, We Adore Thee, I was swept to the back of the church on the arm of my new husband.

I tried to eat around the lump in my throat as I sat at the front of the room facing all the guests as they enjoyed a home cooked meal of my mom's recipes consisting of cheesy potatoes with ham, green sweet peas, fresh dinner rolls, and salad prepared by an Aunt and a few family friends. The meal was followed by a large three-tiered cake with a water fountain in the center and teal roses so bright they turned the mouths of everyone who partook a less than pretty dark green.

When it was time to leave, the photographer followed us out to our car to capture our leaving with a few more photos. What followed kept me from bringing our good-bye photos out of hiding for more than two years. The photographer insisted we share a kiss for the camera. Now remember, we had not kissed before. As my new husband leaned in, my eyes practically crossed as I waited with hitched breath. He planted a very nice, chaste kiss upon my barely closed mouth, but dear me couldn't compose myself enough to be romantic and close my eyes. The photographer chuckled and exclaimed, "Katie, you're supposed to close your eyes!" With pink tinged cheeks, we went for round two which proved successful. I could not get out of that church parking lot fast enough.

*   *   *   *   *

When someone else's happiness is your happiness, that is love.
~ Lana Del Rey

Reset

I can't change the direction of the wind, but I can adjust my sails to always reach my destination. ~ Jimmy Dean

On our wedding night, I began to cry gut-wrenching sobs that didn't cease for hours. Today my heart breaks for what my sweet husband endured that night. It was incredibly unfair to him. He was a perfect gentleman, holding me as I cried.

I cried for youth lost, confusion about where I fit in this new life I had fallen into, and overwhelmed with the responsibility to make my new husband happy.

*   *   *   *   *

The following morning, we left on an airplane. It was a strange sensation indeed to hold hands, but by the end of the day, my fingers felt weird when they weren't intertwined with my husband's.

In the two weeks that followed, my level of comfort in being myself with him blossomed. He did not like all of it. He was thirty and two weeks. I was eighteen and seven months. The maturity level was unequal to say the least.

Over the next two weeks, as we flew to beautiful places across the country, I would cry at night over the fact that my flaws were showing themselves clearly and that even my new husband didn't like part of the person he was getting to know.

*   *   *   *   *

Soon after our wedding, Ivan stated that he didn't know why, but he just couldn't cherish me. Our vows stated that we'd love and cherish until death us do part, but it was proving to be impossible. I was devastated, but I knew it was my fault entirely. Ivan was smart, strong, and good. I was not.

Six months after our wedding, the church we belonged to started to crumble, and soon its doors were closed permanently. While visiting a little church in a small town I'd never been to before, I listened as the preacher talked of God and the love that He is and has for me. Like so many times before, I responded to the invitation to go forward to receive prayer.

But this time a literal warmth poured over my broken heart. Tears like so many times before washed over my cheeks, but hope crept in where despair had always lingered. My heart was enveloped in an overwhelming feeling of love unlike any feeling I had ever experienced before. Healing washed over me and bathed me in light. It bathed my heart in light. As this all-encompassing loved filled my being, the cracks in my heart filled with light and drove out the forsaken darkness I'd lived with since my youth.

I had been afraid of God, but this new experience revealed to me a God of love, light, healing, and peace. It was a defining moment in my life. The lenses with which I looked at the world changed

colors, and where they were fuzzy, they became clear.

* * * * *

"Let the morning bring me word of your unfailing love, ... "
~ Psalm 143:8 (NIV)

Transition and Motherhood

Our love of being right is best understood as our fear of being wrong. ~ Kathryn Schulz

The harshness of the church environment growing up where He was depicted as an angry, waiting to pounce if I misstepped God fell away as He began to write His laws on my heart, though I had yet to fully understand.

As the laws of man fell away, I was left reeling without the direction I'd always relied on. It was a new and uncomfortable place to be. While I was ever so hungry, with the rules and regulations I'd grown up with suddenly lifted, I was a bit like sheep left suddenly without a shepherd.

My goal isn't to suggest that our lead ministers were wrong, but simply to share how my life took a different path, the right one for me. Many of the hard things in my life served to bring me to the place of knowing God on a personal level. Not according to man's standard of holiness, but coming to Him just as I am and knowing His voice with a very personal relationship.

God began to write His laws on my heart, and much of the fear that came from constantly looking for demons and sin in my heart and surroundings began to melt away. As fear dissipated, peace in my heart grew.

*   *   *   *   *

Ivan and I fumbled our way through the first seventeen months of marriage. Some good moments, some bad. Some sweet, some pain filled, I couldn't wait to have four or six children, so I was delighted when the pregnancy test was positive. After two weeks of morning sickness, I enjoyed every single moment of carrying the gift of child who insisted on nestling up into my ribs, right under my heart.

*   *   *   *   *

My beautiful daughter, Kara, arrived just after our second anniversary. I was immediately in love, but I was completely unprepared for the emotional journey that followed. I cried every night for two weeks following her birth.

Ivan worked out of town every week for six months out of the year. For the next few months, I'd pack coolers of food for him to take for the week, send him off, lock the door and, crawl into bed if Kara was still asleep, or I'd curl up in a ball on the couch. The days passed in a fog. I worried for years that I didn't bond enough with her because I was emotionally unavailable.

Over the summer, I gradually got back into life.

*   *   *   *   *

What bond Ivan and I had created dissolved as time passed. I couldn't please him. I felt criticized for being me and everything that entailed. Today I realize that while I loved him and sought to please him, I disrespected him in ways I was unaware of, and the pain ran just as deep for him.

Four years into our marriage, each evening with my husband and child sleeping, I'd tiptoe into the bathroom, lock the door, and fall apart. Alone, I cried until there were no tears, and then I cried some more. Was there no hope? Was my marriage over? My hearts cry was, "Where are you God?" I didn't know if He was real. I was taught many things about God, but I came to the place where I questioned His existence. I called my former pastor to seek his advice. He compassionately told me that he didn't know how to help me.

Out of desperation, seeking to stay above the sea of despair that sought to swallow me, I booked three nights at a motel in town. Those days passed in a blur. At the end of the third day, when the time came for me to return to our home, I couldn't bring myself to go back. It held only painful memories.

My family stepped in to help care for my daughter in a way I'm eternally grateful for. My mom became Kara's favorite person.

While I loved my daughter with all I had, my heart was so numb I could barely take care of myself.

*   *   *   *   *

I rented a room at my parent's house and got a job as a waitress at a local Italian restaurant, tentatively opening this quiet mouth, initiating conversation at each table that I served. For the next five months, I poured myself into serving people coffee, water, and food. That much I could do with abandon.

Over the next few months, I received some clarity. I never lost sight of the fact that I loved Ivan, but I didn't know how to fix things. I expressed my desire to Ivan that I wanted to come back. He was cautious and careful. I knew I didn't have peace to move back in with him yet, but I went back. Did it work? No, I moved too soon. He wasn't ready for me, and maybe I wasn't ready either, though I wanted to be. After a few months, I decided to move into one of our guest bedrooms. In the same house by day, and alone by night. I knew and understood that Ivan didn't want me, and probably more accurately, didn't dare trust his heart to me.

* * * * *

She loved so much, she lost herself. ~ Unknown

13

Lost Found and Angel Babies

I loved you like there was no tomorrow, and then suddenly there wasn't. ~ Unknown

During that hopeless season of there being little chance of our marriage surviving, I'd been going to clubs with friends. The one avenue of freedom for my wounded heart was the chance to dance with wild abandon which gave my heart emotional release to a degree I had no idea existed. Each time I danced until closing time.

Soon after, while going out to have drinks with friends, I was asked to meet at a mutual gathering place by a casual acquaintance I'd met a few years earlier. I went knowing that I was leftover goods with a nice personality, so it didn't occur to me that I was being pursued. My dating experience was nil. With my heart wounded to the point that I didn't expect it to be repaired, I boldly went all by myself to this gathering place.

Eric was attentive. He seemed to like me a lot, which I found intoxicating. I can't say that I was attracted to him, but for a man to desire me was like balm to an oozing wound. We danced in the way of conversation. He led, I followed. He asked me to take a ride, and I went with him. The night ended as I now know is to be expected, with a casual joining of bodies for a moment. Healing salve to my wounded soul. The night embraced me as moonlight crept into the cracks of my fractured being. I went home in a daze.

The next morning dawned, and I felt alive. I felt valid. Somebody wanted me. The sunshine was brighter, and the air felt cleaner. I felt like a bird newly released from a cage, free to fly.

With little sleep, I went about my work week with a spring in my step. After all, why would I need sleep when I had boundless energy from finding out that I was desirable. I mattered.

Eric didn't know me well, but what little he knew, he wanted more of me. What a strange feeling. I suddenly wanted to take on the world.

Upon seeing Eric the following week, I noticed that he appeared reserved. I found this strange. I was in a newly discovered arena, bubbly and vivacious for the first time in my life.

My heart dropped a bit. Disappointed, I pondered what could've happened? Why was he withdrawing?

Oh, was I more a conquest than a love interest? Did I really not hold more worth than bragging rights to his prowess? Maybe I wasn't wanted after all.

*   *   *   *   *

While helping my dad paint the interior of a house as I often did growing up, I found an apartment and moved into town, ready to do life on my own.

A few months later, Ivan filed for divorce. This changed everything for me because I knew he'd be okay. He would live life without me, and he'd be just fine. Up to this point, I carried so much guilt for not being enough wife for him that I responded to him and life from guilt instead of choosing to live life with purpose.

For the first time ever, I saw him as a man who was his own and not my husband. I was a woman who was her own. No pressure, just being ourselves on our own. I found that I really liked him and wanted to be with him, but I didn't have the courage to pursue him since I didn't expect our relationship to ever be repaired.

In the meantime, we attended co-parenting classes and were one class away from our divorce being finalized when Ivan and I casually began to discuss the matters of our heart when meeting each other to pick up or drop Kara off. Over the next few months, we developed a bond, listening to each other's hearts and thoughts. It was like dating. We slowly built on this new plane. We started over, and I went home to our house. Our place. Us.

*　*　*　*　*

A month later, out of the blue, a friend called me to ask if it was true that I had had one night stands with so and so and five other guys. Utter devastation. Hide, Deny, Protect was my immediate response, "No! No! No! Not true," I replied. Today, I realize that it would've been better for me to say, that is none of your business, or I could've said a small portion of that is true, but I couldn't yet stand up for me.

I waited for Ivan to come home from work and asked him to sit down to talk. With great trepidation, I told him what had transpired months earlier. He was devastated. He got together with some of his friends that evening and told them what I'd done. Humble pie for this girl who was taught all her life that what she had done was wrong, immoral, and unacceptable.

Realizing that Ivan may choose to end our marriage after all and truly believing that I didn't have a right to dispute any decision he made, I went to sleep on the couch.

When he came home, he told me to come to bed.

The following morning, we discussed the future of our relationship over breakfast. I asked him what he wished to do. He stated that we'd had such a wonderful time together over the past month since I'd moved back home that he'd like to continue building our relationship.

Hope whispered that just maybe our marriage had a chance.

I began to choose him and us. Where I had hidden and protected myself from him, I began to open my heart to him. Cautiously, I tiptoed, having no idea of the length of the journey life held for our hearts to be truly joined as one, undivided.

*   *   *   *   *

Shortly after our reconciliation, I discovered I was pregnant. I was delighted, but Ivan was not. He in fact was really upset. Understandably so, since our relationship was tried, but not yet tested. He was trying to trust that we'd go the distance, but there was no way of knowing if we would.

I was sick for the duration of the pregnancy. On the couch sick, while Ivan was working on a sink fixture, I was trying to convince him to be happy that we had a baby on the way, when suddenly, there was a spontaneous rushing of fluid. I frantically ran for the bathroom, wailing as I went, for I knew instinctively that I was losing my baby.

Overwhelming guilt invaded my every waking moment. I was sure that Ivan not wanting a baby and by me being who I was, it was our fault that I lost this baby.

With fresh heartbreak, I waited the weekend through as my body did its work expelling the life I so desperately wanted, but wasn't mine to keep. All passed in due time.

As time went on, I still felt pregnant. I made an appointment with my doctor. During the ultrasound, I was able to see a fluttering heartbeat of a tiny new life. The doctor said everything looked good. I returned home with gladness in my heart, excited for the new promise.

Shortly after, my body expelled a fleeting little life again. A pregnancy test confirmed that I was no longer pregnant. I put the pain away in my heart alone and left it there for six years.

A year and a half later, I received my rainbow baby (a baby that is born following a miscarriage, stillbirth, neonatal death, or infant loss), Ty, a sweet balm for my soul.

During this time, I was searching for God. I wanted to know that he was real beyond what a book said and or what I was taught.

*   *   *   *   *

Not all wounds are so obvious, walk gently in the lives of others.
~ Anonymous

14

Redemption

In order to love who you are, you cannot hate the experiences that shaped you. ~ Andrea Dykstra

As time passed, after the doors of my church closed, I lived in a place between religion and not knowing whether God really existed. For a number of years, I was scared to voice my doubts, because according to my upbringing, it was sacrilegious to even give voice to the questioning of God's existence.

The truth was that I had been instilled with religion all my life, but it left me cold and desolate.

I had a picture of what I perceived to be an angry God with glimpses of some gentle characteristics due to my dad teaching me to talk to God as a friend.

I lived with condemnation for questioning God's existence. The "bathing my heart in love" experience I had in the little country church I visited a few years before was an event that I looked back on with curiosity, but it faded from my view to the point where I felt I may have imagined it. My darkest life moments came after that day, with the time of my separation from Ivan being the darkest of all.

I was desperate to be convinced of God's existence. I sought Him for years. Year after year, my heart cried for a being that it wanted to return to, but I was left despaired from seeking and not finding as I asked Him to show me Him.

In looking back over that time, I can see two sets of footprints when I thought there was only one.

As time passed, I stumbled through confusion with the old ways I was taught and the new path my heart was being compelled to follow.

Gradually, the Lover of my soul began to win my heart and convince me that He was indeed at my side through it all, through no merit of mine.

*   *   *   *   *

He had received me as His daughter, and when I would but open my eyes, He was ever so willing to lavish His affections on me.

He won my heart without the Bible I was raised reading and believing was the only way to know Him and understand who He was. He came to me in the dark of night and asked me if I would follow Him to the ends of the earth. The beautiful gift in this was that when I began reading the Bible again, the words became life, and I recognized them as truth by His Spirit within me.

What if I opened my heart wide and trusted it to this God who loved me so intimately, so unreserved? What if I trusted Him to lead me past the borders set up by man, no holds barred, reckless abandon? I'd been warned by preachers in the past that to choose so was dangerous. Could I turn my heart over to Him to this extent?

His love convinced me of Him and His realness in a way that all the hard preaching I'd ever heard never did. His love created the desire to live right, do well, and live authentically.

* * * * *

As my heart grew in love, the thoughts and accusations I lived with from my youth receded. His boundless love won my heart. I will live in that love all the days of my life.

Knowing that I'm loved in this way convinced me that I'm accepted and completely taken in. Nothing I've done is unredeemable. My confidence grew, and I cared less about what others thought of me. I cared not so much that I didn't weigh what I should. Where I'd had a tremendous fear of others not approving of me, confidence that it didn't matter if others liked me or not grew.

As I gave myself a break, my capacity to love others expanded. I'm not perfect, and that's okay. God met me in the darkest corners of my heart. He's okay with what was there, and now so am I. He replaced the pain that crippled me with His love. He scooped out the broken pieces, leaving behind the essence of His perfect love.

No need to live in pretense. I'm me. There's no one like me. This is good, for were I to live as someone else, the unique person I am would never truly be. My story would never be told because I wouldn't have written it. I've been every person. I'm human. I'm no more than anyone else, but more importantly, I've realized that I'm no less than anyone either. I'm valued as the least of these and as the greatest of these.

* * * * *

Having confidence in who I'm to be creates room for others to feel comfortable to be exactly who they're to be.

In a world where most attempt to copy the look and habits of others, what if I was to be me? What kind of life will I create? What legacy will I leave behind if I live true to who I am?

To be authentic is of incredible importance to me. Therefore, I own my life, the good the bad and the ugly.

If I have nothing to be ashamed of, I will be ashamed of nothing.

I've been to the darkest, most hidden places in my heart, and I came out alright. There was nothing so dark that the light of His love couldn't redeem.

*   *   *   *   *

I will hold myself to a standard of grace, not perfection. ~ Emily Ley

Finding My Footing

I wondered if that was how forgiveness budded; not with the fanfare of epiphany, but with pain gathering its things, packing up, and slipping away unannounced in the middle of the night.
~ Khalid Hosseini

L ife is nothing if not lonely. How many times do we try to fill the lonely moments with noise to distract ourselves?

When a relationship ends, we rush into another one because it's too hard to sit with the loneliness. It's oh so hard to wait.

As hard as it is to admit, there were moments when lonely hurt so intensely during my separation from Ivan that I made an appointment with my chiropractor for an adjustment just for the human contact. I realize today that it's ever so important to surround ourselves with friends we trust to look out for us when our lives are in a state of acute loneliness. Without a support group, loneliness creates vulnerability to the point that a person makes unwise decisions because they're convinced they are cast aside and of little value. We grasp for love in whatever measure we can attain it.

At the same time, loneliness can be just as painful when in an unfulfilling relationship, when even in the same room, your hearts are thousands of miles apart from each other. You're with a person physically, but you know your hearts are not safe in each other's hands because both people hurt so much that it feels safer to live together, alone.

*   *   *   *   *

From early childhood, there were moments when my heart mourned the absence of a tangible presence that my young mind couldn't find words to describe what or who it was.

When my youngest son Ty started school, I felt intense pressure to start a career. The problem was that I hadn't a clue what that was or what it'd look like. I was tempted to get a job as a waitress or do housecleaning, but I knew myself well enough to know if I started either, it'd take the pressure off of me, and in ten years, I'd still be doing the same thing. There's not a thing wrong with either. I enjoyed the seasons in my life when I did both of those things, but I wanted more. As uncomfortable as it was, I forced myself to remain without a title for a time. I described myself as a Jill-of-all-trades. In this season, I catered weddings, cleaned our rental properties, volunteered at school, began online classes to become an aromatherapist, processed the painful moments from childhood, all the while seeking my career and what it might be.

I came to the place where I was okay without a title.

What this season highlighted for me was when asked who we are, we respond with what we do.

I might say, "Hi, my name is Kate, I'm a writer." If I answered with who I am, I'd tell you that I'm at times neurotic. I'm stubborn when it comes to trying new things, but the positive side to that is once I set my mind to something, I'm like a bull dog, and although you might attempt to convince me to give up, I will not. End of story.

I'm passionate about living my life purpose, not leaving this earth until I've lived it all. I seek to live authentically and bring out the best in others. I actively seek to make a moment in the lives of the people I encounter each day a little bit brighter. I'm loved by some beautiful people.

I'm strong, but find it challenging to allow myself to be vulnerable, but I'm getting better at it. In fact, I'm finding that there's strength in being vulnerable. Occasionally dropping the mask and allowing others to see our struggles and that it's ok that we don't have it all figured out yet connects the raw, real, and true for a moment.

While there may be times that we'd beg someone to tell us the short version of who they are, my point is that if we'd but lift the curtain that we so often hide behind, we may be surprised by how alike we all really are.

What if we discover that the world is a bit less lonely when we choose to be real, true, and open?

How many times are we asked how we're doing and we respond with, "good?" How many times are we crying inside, but we can't let anyone see that.

During some of the most painful moments in my childhood, I accepted the lie that I couldn't trust anyone, so I had to do life alone and rely on me to protect me.

Distrust made for many lonely moments in my life. I convinced myself that life was safer with a wall surrounding my heart. While it was safer, I wasn't living, wholly.

While I lived in my own safe world in which I sought to control everything, I withheld the best part of me from those I loved. Believing that I was safe was an illusion, for didn't I spend my childhood in fear of everything around me?

I've contemplated keeping the wall around my heart high, for to lower it means it'll get trampled on. But time after time, I'm reminded that while it may be safer to keep the wall in place, to experience the greatest high, one must allow the lowest low. I've found that it's better to have loved and lost than to never have loved at all. In the healing of heartbreak, one's capacity to love grows greater.

The truth is that while I can't trust everyone, I can give everyone the chance to earn my trust and in that have beautiful moments where my heart is impacted and changed forever.

*   *   *   *   *

Be who you needed when you were younger.

16

Walls Crumbling

He ran His hands over my past – lingering over the dents and worn edges of my heart, and when I thought He'd run away like all the others had…He told me I was a warrior, and that I'd never fight another battle alone. ~ Alfa

The year I gave birth to my son Ty brought a lot of first's. I moved to another state and began to develop my own talents.

For the first month of Ty's life, he and I spent each night on a reclining couch surrounded by piles of pillows so that my sleep deprived body could attempt to catch up.

During all hours of the night, I saw every cooking show that the food channel played. I devoured its contents and began to cook with abandon. The memories from childhood of how my beautiful mother turned me loose in the kitchen to cook beginning at age nine came flooding back Although, my first solo attempt at cooking was a complete flop visually, and I got teased about it for years, (all with good intent) it tasted good, and I was proud of my accomplishment. It was the one area of personal skill that I was happy with growing up. I loved creating new recipes.

With my newly reawakened passion, I entertained often, eager to share new recipes with friends and family. As passion for cooking flowed through my veins, so did the painful events I'd so carefully constructed a wall around.

Memories of angel babies wrenched from my heart before I had a chance to hold them and the buried memories of forbidden hands violating secret places branded my heart with shame. I carried extra body weight for protection, but condemnation for choosing to take care of myself in this way.

That summer, long buried memories began to resurface. For the first week, I would try to allow the memories to return, but each time opened a little, my heart began to race and anxiety overwhelmed me, and I couldn't breathe, so I pushed back.

But one day, I allowed the emotions and memories to rush in. I closed my bedroom door, crawled into bed, curled up into a ball, and hugged my pillow. Words failed me. Instead, quiet groans vibrated in my chest. My nose burned as tears begin to roll uninhibited down my reddening cheeks.

For many years, my heart was closed off from need of others. I couldn't need. I had to go it alone. I helped others, but I alone helped me. The bitterness inside ate away at the flesh of my heart. I longed to feel the warmth of the sun on my face and the summer breeze on my skin, but alas, in the secret most places of my heart, the pain turned hate filled my being to the point that it crowded out peace.

Healing is the hardest part of dealing with a tattered heart. To heal is to feel. The cracks of my long-fractured heart widened as emotions long unchecked loosed their white-knuckle grip.

Bitterness melted away as love flowed in. Pain wracked my body.

The wounds were jagged. Breaths came in gasps. I hugged myself as I rocked back and forth searching for words, but there were none. Only ragged, quivering breaths and moans, desperate for relief.

My body shook as I struggled to catch my breath. I wanted to stop remembering but memories returned of a dimly lit room and dull brown paneled walls. I was laying on old blankets and felt fingers groping. I whimpered for my mom, but she wasn't there. Where was my mom? He finished and pulled me off the bed and carried me down the stained oak stairs. We joined the other few on the main floor. I couldn't speak, for I was too young for more than a few words. I had put this incident on a shelf in my heart, for life goes on. Albeit altered, a portion of innocence was lost. I shouldn't know or remember, but I do.

I have every right to be angry at the injustice of it all. Will anger serve me, or will it swallow me whole? Will I seek justice, or will I extend grace where wrath is deserved?

I laid on my bed emotionally spent. My heart raw, but still beating. My eyes dry, though still red.

I got up and cleaned my kitchen. My son woke from his nap, and I hugged and fed him. Holding him as he nestled his head in the crook of my neck brought peace to my soul.

* * * * *

For the next week, each day repeated itself. Tears, remembering, hurting. I sought peace, but it escaped me.

On the seventh day, I rose the hour before dawn. I sat in the quiet, feeling, seeking, praying, waiting.

In my mind's eye, I saw my predator as a broken little boy. I received a glimpse of the man he would've been before evil encapsulated his being, overtaking the innocence he once embodied.

The pain faded and healing came. Love replaced the anguish. Where the pain was before, peace now flows from my heart.

I am now the strong one. I'm stronger than that which sought to squelch my spirit, to eat me up with the bitterness of the cup which sought to poison my soul, to convince me that I'm unapproachable, unacceptable, unredeemable. I rise. I win. I decide the outcome, and I choose life!

The world is washed anew. I love a little deeper. My family gets to have a bigger piece of my heart, moving ever closer to loving with unrestrained abandon. Not hiding, not denying. Open, honest, and peaceful.

A cure is as though it never was. Healing is gratitude that remains for the experience that created the scar. There's a time for pain, anger, and bitterness, but over time, it eats away at our body and our health. Love heals. Hate breeds disease, and disease robs us of life force.

For every time you've been hurt and your spirit has been crushed, allow love to seep into the crevices that pain has created in your heart. What little light there may be will grow as we let love in. Light drives out darkness. Hate is driven out as light flows in.

*   *   *   *   *

It is harder to talk about what was done to me than the things I've done. The things I did were the choices I made whether right or wrong.

That unspeakable, dirty thing that altered who I should've been poured shame on my soul so that I blamed myself for what was done to me.

Someone told me that a large portion of sexual abuse and or molestation happens within the family circle. While this book isn't about statistics, from the many people I've encountered who have been victims of it, I don't find it difficult to believe. I seem to be more surprised when I learn that someone hasn't been affected by it.

For all the times I've heard this laughed and joked about in social circles, I've questioned how it remains an epidemic. The conclusion I've come to is that it remains a hidden but rampant, secret part of society because the very thing it does is tell those who are touched by it to deny, hide, and protect, whether the victim or abuser. The shame that the victim and abuser carry is designed to rob them of peace permanently.

Where innocence resided, shame infiltrates, destroying the soul and leaving a lasting mark of shame on the victim and abuser alike, thus from generation to generation, it continues. The cycle stops with me. I will shed light on the dark thing, and I shall speak of the hidden things, the shameful things that grow by night.

Where there was shame, light shall pour in. Where there was denial, I speak truth. Where there was no protection because my parents didn't know, I speak up for me now. Little Katie has a voice, and so shall every little boy and girl touched by the mark of this beast.

God's divine love shall flow into the darkest places, scoop up the pain, and leave behind the very essence of His love and healing. Where there was shame, there is now beauty. Where there was denial, it is replaced with boldness to receive the truth that I'm no longer defined by this ugly thing. Instead, I'm redeemed. The stain my soul carried in secret, but was written in my eyes for the world to see, is replaced with wholeness. It is no longer mine to carry. Guilt ceases as His love flows through every broken crevice of my heart, and while some scars show as a memory, the pain is gone, and only gratitude remains for this amazing gift that is restoration.

* * * * *

Regarding sexual molestation, it's such a shameful thing to admit to being a victim to that it seems many women are mistakenly strong supporters of keeping its ugly head intact, maybe more so than men.

I've heard many women's responses to others being sexually abused," She was wearing suggestive clothing." or "She was asking for it." and other such comments. Some of which were my own thoughts before I saw the lies for what they were.

We need to understand that it doesn't matter what a girl or woman is wearing or not wearing, her body is sacred and not to be violated.

Many times, mamas strongly defend their husbands, fathers, brothers, and sons. Understandably so, because they love them with a mother's heart that was designed to nurture, take care of and love well. It can be difficult to admit that the person they love with such abandon could have a seed of that ugly, hidden away thing in their heart to do those unthinkable acts.

It is a flawed view to defend these acts, regardless who committed them. When we shed light on the darkness, it loses its power. When it loses its power, and the truth is brought to light, it can no longer hide.

I have no formal training on sexual abuse and or incest, but I do know that it redefines who you were meant to be. I believe that the reason it continues to run rampant is because it's such a shameful thing. It's made light of and made fun of on a wide scale. The perpetrators hide and bow to its demands as much as the victim does. The spirit of it seeks to kill and destroy. Those who were victims of it many times become predators, helpless to resist the pull of its demonic force. Each perpetrator was once a victim of it.

When the sexual molestation occurred, not only did it change who I was, but the same fear and shame that the perpetrator carried became a part of me. I accepted the lie that I must fear, and I must hide. It was by design of the enemy of my soul to pile lie upon lie on my young heart to steal innocence and destroy truth and convince me in my earliest days that I was flawed and unredeemable.

The truth is that I don't have to carry this guilt and shame. Jesus carried that to the cross for me. The guilt and shame were already paid for long before I was born, but since I didn't know that, the enemy of my soul had the freedom to attempt to drown me with these lies.

Where as a child and youth, I grew in stolen innocence, fear, and shame. Today, I grow in knowing that it wasn't for me to carry. It was simply smoke and mirrors to convince me that it was truth.

*   *   *   *   *

Incest has no respect of persons or of family lineage. It doesn't matter if you have a full bank account or an empty one. It's all the same. I have no formal training in it, but I'm a product of it. I know the pain and shame it holds over those it touches. It grows like an unwanted weed because it returns to grow despite weed killer. It grows despite our hating it. It's a spirit that alights from generation to generation. Only when it's shown the light of day, does the darkness of night desist. ~ Kate Troyer

Walls Crumbling

Light Filled Cracks

Your most profound and intimate experiences of worship will likely be in your darkest days – when your heart is broken, when you feel abandoned, when you're out of options, when the pain is great – and you turn to God alone. ~ Rick Warren

The closer I got to my heart, the more pain I felt and the more I was tempted to run. All the carefully constructed walls began to crack and crumble. I thought of turning back, but the path back disappeared from my vision. The cocoon was not reusable.

As light filled the cracks, they widened. The pain intensified, and the walls of my heart threatened to buckle under the onslaught of feelings that rushed in and out.

Where I tried to run from it, I posed the question to myself,

"Where will you run?" My answer was "I have nowhere to run but inward." I ran to food most of my life. It served me for a season, but then began to punish me for my trust in it.

How strange is it that what I used as a young girl to protect me was in fact an illusion of protection since when I left food out, I discovered it had actually only been covering the things I thought it had settled.

As a child, I ate sugar voraciously because I was desperate for sweet, healing love, but each time the sugar's high dissipated, it left in its wake exhaustion, loneliness, and despair. My heart pursued this illusive love until it awakened to the truth that it was a sham, a sweetness of no lasting substance.

* * * * *

A weed is but an unloved flower. ~ Ella Wheeler Wilcox

Fear Lies and Truth

Gratitude can transform common days into thanksgivings, turn routine jobs into joy, and change ordinary opportunities into blessings. ~ William A. Ward

I discovered about ten years into our marriage that whenever Ivan would say something that hurt my feelings, I would rush to eat something unhealthy. I was shocked when I realized that I in fact sought to hurt me when someone else hurt me. I believed in my heart that I deserved to be hurt and not loved. I fought back, but my way of fighting was to hurt me.

Day by day I began to tune in, noticing that I was doing it. I began to sit with the emotion instead of eating something sweet.

A short time later, I began to eat chips. I can't help but believe that I ate crunchy chips to express long pent up emotions. My experience is that expressing my emotions is healthy for me.

My goal is to get to the place where I replace my way of expression with salty, crunchy foods with something that supports my health long term like daily running or walking, a habit I loved as a young girl.

The most freeing times in my life were when I ran, especially on the school playground when I outran the cutest boy in my class.

*   *   *   *   *

In looking back over my life, I realize that in my mind, I was fat whether I was close to my ideal weight or twenty pounds or more than that. I yo-yo dieted from my teenage years forward. It was a vicious cycle. I'd lose ten pounds, people would compliment me, I'd appreciate it, but the compliments made me feel uncomfortable and unsafe. A few years ago, after losing thirty pounds, I received many positive comments. I panicked, abruptly stopped losing weight, and immediately gained some of it back.

As strange as it may seem, I saw myself the same and felt the same at any weight. It wasn't until I compared photos from my early years of marriage to twenty years later that I realized there was a difference.

*   *   *   *   *

I've gone through periods in my life where I've exercised in the form of power walking or running and enjoyed it immensely.

One day, as I ran past the neighboring farm, I heard their German Shepherd barking. I'd always been scared of dogs, but I saw the owner outside and heard her yelling at the dog, so I trusted that the dog would mind her.

With my earbuds in place and music jamming, I continued past the farm, when suddenly, I heard the owner yell loudly for the dog to get back. I looked straight ahead, thinking that if I ignored the dog it wouldn't bite. Suddenly, I felt the dog bite into the back of my thigh. Just as quickly as it grabbed me, it let go and ran back to its owner. Terrified, and not waiting to talk to the homeowner because I was afraid the dog would come at me again, I quickened my pace and ran the rest of the way home.

I checked the bite and it wasn't bad, just a small puncture wound. I washed the bite with peroxide and applied Amish drawing salve we'd used since I was a little girl.

I immediately grabbed a note card and envelope and sat at the kitchen table to pen a note to the farmer. I told them that while I was shaken badly, I was okay. I received a note from the dog's owner a few days later apologizing for the dog's behavior. Unfortunately, the damage was done.

I tried to go walking again, this time with a stick and in a different direction, but in my mind that dog grew as big as a grizzly bear, and I gave in.

When I go on a walk with my husband or daughter and a dog starts barking, panic sets in immediately. Thankfully, each interaction with a dog since the farmer's dog has been a friendly one.

It is another area that I want to overcome and seize the freedom of the open road again.

* * * * *

Ten years after my son Ty was born, I began to address my health and seek to heal my thyroid that clearly wasn't functioning as designed. The trauma it endured trying to keep up with my survival tactics left it exhausted.

I started processing the pain of losing my babies. I had an especially difficult day filled with tears and physical heart pain. I went to sleep that night and dreamed of a baby boy I realized was the one I lost. The cry of my heart the following day was, "Where are you, my son?" I named him Reagan Eli, Eli after my dad. The following night, I dreamed of a little girl and knew she was my other baby. The previous day repeated itself. Again, my heart's cry was, "Where are you, my daughter?" I named her Ava Sarah, Sarah after my mom.

I went to the store the following day, purchased a blue and a pink balloon, and let them go in my backyard, blessing the children I'd never know on this earth. I watched the balloons until they faded from view. It's been fifteen years, and there are still moments when the memory of them and the impact of their very brief time with me and wondering who they'd be today brings tears to my eyes. I don't know why they couldn't stay, but I'm thankful for the bond I have with my angel babies and the lasting imprint they left on my heart.

*   *   *   *   *

The most powerful moment concerning the state of my health came the day I realized that I had a white-knuckle grip on the fear of judgment concerning sex outside of marriage. I'd been taught from childhood that to have sex outside of marriage was dishonorable and deplorable because the Bible said so.

While it's true that the Bible contains instructions on marriage, what was missing was the human element of what pertained to me at the time, desolation, feeling like leftover goods, and being a most undesirable, broken woman. I never felt judged by God, but I felt judged harshly by people. I discovered the truth that everything is permissible, but everything is not profitable.

In those moments, I became every woman, every person. Where judgment resided due to the teachings I grew up with, grace and compassion for each person who finds themselves in a place they've never been before or have always resided in was imparted. As humbling as it's been to admit I did this, I'm profoundly grateful for the humility that was established in my heart during that difficult season of my life.

It became of great importance to me to teach my children more than just what the Bible says, but also that there are consequences for one's actions, either by those close to us or what is accepted by a culture or by society.

Until that moment, I never considered humbling my heart to the point of admitting what was hidden away in it.

That day, I realized as hard as I held it desperately hidden, my body couldn't release the excess weight because I needed it to protect me.

In that moment, I knew that if I had nothing to be ashamed of, I would be ashamed of nothing. I can let go of it all. I can let peace replace fear and let the pieces fall where they may. The more I let go of the fear of judgment, the more peace fills the places judgment previously held.

When I stand in judgment of others, I'll see judgment staring back at me.

*   *   *   *   *

I was raised in a church environment that instilled the importance of rising quickly to judgment, lest the dark places of my heart be shone in the light of day, and its proven that the very thing I'm judging resides in my heart also.

Judgment from those who claimed to care about my soul drove me to the outer courts for a season, asking how I could have made the choices I made after all I was taught, but I hold no ill will for those who reacted with judgment, for I myself have been the greatest of judges.

It was love and compassion that changed my heart and the direction of my life. It was overwhelming, heart-hugging love by the God who proved Himself a redeemer of the dark places and the One who visited the most secret place of my heart, saw what was there, and loved me just the same. What He found didn't change His acceptance of me anymore than if He only found purest, whitest snow.

His all-encompassing love won my heart and my allegiance. Love wins over judgment every time.

* * * * *

Life becomes easier when you learn to accept an apology you never get. ~ Robert Brault

Fear Lies and Truth

19

Caterpillar to Butterfly

One day she finally grasped that unexpected things were always going to happen in life. And with that she realized the only control she had was how she chose to handle them. So she made the decision to survive using, courage, humor, and grace. She was the queen of her life and the choice was hers. ~ Lupytha Hermin

Trying to fit the mold of marriage and relationship as I was taught caused Ivan and I untold heartache. The more I sought to defer my dreams to match his, the more frustrated I became and the more difficult it was for both of us.

I tried for years to get him to dream and build with me, to create a mutual legacy. He had what he wanted, but since I didn't and thought I had to keep in line with what he wanted, I came to resent his refusal to dream with me. In my fortieth year, I embarked on my new journey. I was willing to live within our marriage, even if alone, to find what I was created for.

Imagine my surprise, when the glasses I looked at life through changed completely. I suddenly realized that there are no limits. Ivan may not like everything I choose to do, but I was okay with it. For years, I didn't want what he chose, but I tried to force myself to accept it.

When I gave myself the freedom to be me and began to dream of the life I wanted to create, the dynamic of our relationship changed dramatically. Instead of trying to push what I perceived was an elephant in the room out, I gave this elephant it's spot and dreamed anyway. In so doing, our relationship became a place of peace.

I didn't need someone to rescue me. I needed to become the strong woman I am on my own. That's not to say that I haven't had amazing people in my corner, but had Ivan been the man I thought I needed for a long time, I wouldn't have fought so hard for freedom from the shell I lived in. Had I had everything given to me, I would've been more likely to stay a caterpillar.

The times that it felt that Ivan opposed all that I wanted worked in my favor. Just as being overweight compelled me to seek approval outside of societal acceptance, so the misunderstandings in our relationship compelled me to find what brought peace to me and peace for our marriage.

The drawing of the path I felt inclined to follow made the cocoon uncomfortable enough that I was desperate to forge ahead, for to remain in the cocoon was more difficult than to face the scary prospect of opening my wings and learning to fly. Thus, I left the warmth of its incredibly tight and constricting small space to experience the world unbound and unshackled.

* * * * *

Ivan has always said that what first attracted him to me was my sweet spirit. He liked me from the time I was fourteen, but he had to wait for me to grow up to seek a relationship.

He likes to say he had a hand in raising me since he was my dad's hired hand from the time I was about two years old, but I think he quickly changed his mind. We both belonged to the same church and had heard all that a woman was supposed to be, and from what he observed, I fit the bill almost perfectly. After he married me, he realized that he didn't know me at all. Thus, reconsidering his admission to having a hand in raising me.

In discovering that behind my carefully constructed curtain was a broken young woman who was quite unprepared for marriage and unequally matched in maturity, proved to challenge his professed love for me to a great degree.

I'm profoundly grateful for the amazing man I get to call my husband.

For the moments throughout our years together that I thought our marriage may have been a mistake, I'm thankful that our relationship, even if it started out less than ideal, was redeemable. Feeling butterflies in your stomach at the sight of the man you love after ten, twenty, or more years together may be even sweeter than experiencing them in the beginning of the relationship.

The most beautiful gift I've received concerning my relationship with my husband is realizing that unconditional love is having disagreements, different goals, and different views in life, but at the end of the day, accepting the other person entirely for all those things.

After many years of struggling, it's a beautiful gift to have as much confidence in my abilities to do life as I used to have in his abilities, when I was incredibly intimidated by my strong, much wiser husband who was the first to tell me that his way of doing things was the right way. He's discovered that my way is right, too. At least that's what I tell him. Wink.

*   *   *   *   *

In the beginning of our relationship, as was strongly instructed by the church of my teenage years, I asked Ivan permission for most everything I did. For a season, it worked for us flawlessly, but as I began to grow and develop the ability to think for myself, I

111

experienced years of frustration within my subjected position that caused us both a lot of stress, coming to the realization that this way was not right for either of us. I began to take my place in life and in our relationship with confidence.

The beginning of our relationship was more like a father, daughter relationship than a mutual joining of two hearts who go through life together.

There were many areas in my life that Ivan couldn't shed light on, just as I couldn't see everything from his point of view. One reason being, his mind doesn't work like mine, and life affects a woman differently than a man.

I married him with the mistaken idea that he'd be my knight in shining armor, hug me so tight that all the broken pieces would be glued together again, but we both brought baggage to our relationship needing to be rescued in a way that another human being cannot provide.

I came to realize that he couldn't complete me as I thought he would and should, and when I became whole on my own, he complemented my heart beautifully.

Today, we frequently discuss our thoughts and at times disagree, but I've found it to be of great benefit to me, for we can always go far enough to find someone to agree with us, but it's the conversations that challenge us that either change our perspective or deepen our faith in something we believe.

I was created to be a strong woman. One who thinks for herself and lives life per her personal convictions. One who carves out a life for herself, one her husband can respect and trust. A help meet for him, not a daughter.

I'm grateful that my husband values my opinions, my thoughts on issues that arise, and expresses full confidence and appreciation in my rearing of our children.

I value what I share with Ivan immensely. He will never be taken advantage of, but he's loyal and has been the perfect man to stand beside me as I blossom into the woman I am today. There were times when I desperately wanted him to refute the lies I believed about myself, but he simply stood by supporting my journey from caterpillar to butterfly.

I couldn't have accepted a marriage proposal from anyone better suited for me than him.

*   *   *   *   *

Courage doesn't not always roar, sometimes courage is the quiet voice at the end of the day saying, I will try again tomorrow.
~ Mary Anne Radmacher

20

No is A Good Word

Life is tough my darling, but so are you. ~ Stephanie Bennett Henry

One of the ways that sexual molestation left a lasting imprint on my heart for most of my life was that it robbed me of knowing that I'm allowed to say no. Being violated early in life taught me that I have no power and that I must please to appease. I have no right to say no, and if I don't please, I won't be loved.

In any situation I found myself in, if someone asked for something, I gave it to them. Whether it was a personal treasure or if it was asking me to help them do something, I couldn't say no.

Today, it brings me to tears when I look back on the vulnerable younger Katie who saw herself of so little value that even when she was uncomfortable with a man invading her space, she couldn't speak up or stand up for herself. Instead, she turned the anger and shame inward.

I was taught all my life that the Bible says this and the Bible says that, but it instilled nothing of lasting impact when I found myself in a season where I questioned whether God was real or not.

Much emphasis was put on outward covering of the body in the environment I grew up in, first in the Amish church, where women were to cover their heads with the Amish cap and wear a dress that covered the neck all the way to the ankles, then a type of Mennonite church in my teen years.

*   *   *   *   *

In the church of my teen years, modesty in a woman was preached about often. As I sat in church service one Sunday morning, the preacher pointed me out to the congregation as being an example

116

of courage and modesty because I was wearing a white dress that covered my neck all the way down to my ankles.

This was incredibly uncomfortable because I didn't like being the center of attention, and it wasn't the first time I was pointed out as being an example of a good young woman. It caused some of the girls in the church to resent me and made friendship difficult, and the attention put on the outward appearance made for the illusion of a perfect young girl if she dressed a certain way. It didn't reveal the wounded spirit residing within and the cry for love and acceptance.

The focus of covering a woman's body outwardly provided the look of holiness that was encouraged and preached about often, but it made the wearing of a tattered, broken dress of shame and guilt in my heart invisible.

The mantra that played in my mind at every moment I was in public, "Breath quietly." "Pull your stomach in." "Don't Draw attention to yourself." "Walk slow and step gently or you'll look fatter." took up so much of my waking thoughts that it didn't allow for thoughts of the future outside of the ingrained acceptance to get married and have children soon.

Growing up with the opportunity to go further than eighth grade not being an option, I never gave thought to a life outside of marriage and children.

*   *   *   *   *

During my separation from Ivan, a mutual married friend who pretended to care about my well-being, tried numerous times to get me to go with him. I pretended I didn't notice until one night he touched me inappropriately. I felt violated and betrayed, but I couldn't stand up for myself. I felt incredibly ashamed, so I pretended it never happened. Instead, I went home and cried, but from that time on, I made sure to avoid being alone with him at all cost.

It would probably seem obvious to many reading this that I put myself in vulnerable positions, so what happened was my fault. Yes, I did make unwise choices, but my experiences that summer taught me very quickly that I had to surround myself with people I trusted and with people who truly valued my well-being, emotionally, mentally, and physically when I'm in an unsure place in life.

I've heard comments not meant for my ears concerning newly separated or divorced women and the desperation they feel to be assured that they're not leftover goods. I may have glossed over it, had I not found the truth of that statement in my own life. I found that when I needed protection most, there were men who sought to take advantage of my state. Although I'm sure that many times men are just as hungry for validation and respect.

I freely admit my part in what took place that summer, but had I known that I was a woman of value, it most likely would never have happened. I mistakenly thought that being wanted by a man meant I was valued.

I respect any man who given the opportunity to be with a vulnerable woman, shows her respect and reminds her that she's a woman of value and deserves being treated as a treasure.

*   *   *   *   *

Today, I still find it difficult to tell others when I don't like something, but I'm growing little by little.

The gift in the rude awakening I had in that season of my life is that while it was a painful season, it taught me the importance of teaching my children of the consequences of our choices.

I was taught everything not to do, but I wasn't taught what to do.

I understand that in many religious circles, telling people what the Bible says is expected to be enough to keep a person from making unwise choices, but I learned firsthand that when in an unsteady place in life, this expectation holds no water at all.

When I realized that I'm loved and enough just as I am, I learned that I can say no, and it won't make me any less accepted.

I'm truly grateful for restoration, for to have the pain of rejection and the feeling of leftover goods be turned into peace in every area of my heart is an eternal gift of untold value.

May we teach our daughters that they are of great value, and that a man must slay dragons to prove worthy of being with her.

May we teach our sons to respect a woman, see her as a person of unmeasured value rather than an object, even when she doesn't know that truth herself.

*   *   *   *   *

Someone I loved once gave me a box full of darkness. It took me years to understand that this, too, was a gift. ~ Mary Oliver

No is A Good Word

21

Unlovable

We're stronger in the places that we've been broken. ~ Ernest Hemingway

I t is when we're the hardest to love that we need it the most. Oh, how well I know this truth. It's in the darkest night, when we feel the prickliest, that compassion means the most and yet it is the most difficult time to receive it. We so often react to kindness with the judgment we put on ourselves and tend to project that judgment on those seeking to get past our prickly exterior.

In one of the darkest moments of my relationship with Ivan, I confessed that while I loved him, I didn't know if I had it in me to be vulnerable enough to allow my heart the capacity to open it's cracked exterior to him one more time. I wanted to retreat. I wanted to be alone more than I wanted to fight for us. It was too hard. It hurt too much. It seemed it would be easier to go live somewhere alone where no one knew me.

By looking through the lenses of pain, everything Ivan said hurt me. I received what he said by the glasses I looked through instead of how he meant it.

Early in our marriage, I had mentioned to Ivan that I had considered pursuing a singing career. His response was a person had to be good to do that, confirmed my belief that I wasn't good enough was true.

I later realized that he had barely heard me sing. He didn't know what my voice sounded like. It was with such little effort that anyone had the ability to persuade me that I couldn't achieve something I was interested in. I really wanted him to encourage me to try it, but encouragement wasn't for him to give me.

There were many instances in our relationship that I wanted him to give me life. I wanted him to refute the lies I believed about me, but it wasn't his to give me. It was for me to know, discover, and realize.

*   *   *   *   *

One day, while feeling particularly bad about myself, I mentioned trying a new exercise plan that required buying new exercise equipment. Ivan's question of would I use it long term or quit as I had with every other thing I'd tried resulted in a major breakdown for me. I walked away quickly, retreating to the privacy of the big, red, now empty barn on our property before I burst into tears.

I found a soft spot in the hayloft to fall into and let fear and criticism pour over my heart, again, agreeing with the truths of inadequacy I long held.

I know today that Ivan's question was entirely justified. I knew it at the time as well, but I couldn't see that there was logic to his response. I could only feel despair, criticism, and hurt.

Today, it makes sense why I was unsuccessful in any weight loss or exercise plan I tried. The core beliefs I held supported me in being as dramatically flawed as possible in my own mind because I firmly believed I didn't deserve better.

* * * * *

From age twelve, when puberty started, I grew fat and couldn't see myself differently until my heart healed from the need to protect myself.

While going through old photos soon after I turned forty, I was amazed when I looked at pictures of me growing up through eyes of love. Tears flowed freely when I realized that I wasn't fat. I wasn't skinny, but I wasn't fat, as I had believed in my mind.

I cried for the judgment the younger me endured. When I should've been my own best friend, I met myself in the mirror each time with criticism and disdain.

With knowing that I didn't have to be perfect, I began to be there for the younger me by answering the voice of her doubts and fears with acceptance. I didn't have to do everything perfectly. In fact, for many years, I was held captive by my demand for perfection. I couldn't do anything perfectly, so I did little.

Where there had been self-loathing, I met the girl in the mirror with a smile. Where there had been criticism, I gave compassion. A small feat for this girl, for to meet me with anything other than disdain challenged everything I'd believed up to this point. In the secret places of my heart, religion had convinced me that to accept myself as enough was foolish pride. I was supposed to accept that Jesus had made me whole, but I had to despise myself at the same time.

To realize that God created me because He desired to have a relationship with me was a marvelous revelation. Coming to the realization that through Jesus I was made flawless and that He delights in me, His beloved daughter was healing balm to my wounded soul.

When God sees me, He sees me through the perfect lens that is Jesus. I'm completely taken in, no holds barred, totally accepted.

To know that I'm embraced wholly and entirely by my Redeemer, my fractured heart, my broken dreams, and my flawed body is life's sweetest gift.

His all-encompassing acceptance of me has wrought adoration of Him unlike all the judgment and efforts to appease Him and please Him brought all those years.

*   *   *   *   *

A candle loses nothing by lighting another candle. ~ James Keller

Beautiful

People do not realize that their opinion of the world is also a confession of their character. ~ Ralph Waldo Emerson

Am I beautiful? Beginning in my teens, this was the question that was deeply embedded within me, the question that I wanted so very much to be answered with a yes. I wanted to be beautiful, even before I knew how to ask, but I felt such a void each time I did. I thought my face looked okay, but that didn't hold any water when I saw the flawed, awkward, young girl whose mental picture of me spoke louder than my eyes.

I spent more time primping my hair than was acceptable for a young Amish girl, carefully putting my covering over my placed, just so, hair bun, so as not to cause my covering to have dents in it, and then returned to my daily obligations.

I spent ample time doing my hair, but to look at myself in the mirror was uncomfortable to a great degree. I refused to get close to the girl that would've looked back at me.

*   *   *   *   *

I deeply value the focus on kindness that Mom instilled in me.

As a child, when I'd come home from school or other social event and told Mom that someone had done something unkind and my feelings had been hurt, she was empathetic but encouraged me to try to see it through the other child's eyes. This evoked in me the desire to feel what others feel and look beyond a person's actions to their heart within.

My mom's reaction to the children who hurt me did more for me than bad mouthing them would have. Her bashing them would have caused me to think they were stronger than me. Instead, she encouraged me to rise above the words.

*　*　*　*　*

Over the years, the apologies I received from friends who stated that they had misused me because they felt jealous of me surprised me greatly. I felt that had they spent a day in my mind, they would've gladly returned to their own.

Growing up, it appeared to others that our family was wealthy because each time my parents saw a need, they would help fill that need. I suppose we were wealthy compared to many other families, but I didn't understand why other children lashed out at me because they thought I had everything, when I didn't benefit from it in the way they thought I did.

First, let me say that I had a comfortable life growing up. My parents provided for me well. I never went hungry and always had a warm place to lay my head.

Mom was quick to help anyone in need and often did without to help others, thus, teaching me the same thing. However, she has frequently apologized for the things we did without because she helped others so much, but I hold no ill feelings about her choices. My mom is the most generous person I know, and I'm proud of her.

I observed church leaders tell my parents about a need in the church because they knew my parents wouldn't hesitate for a second to help, but then turn around and tell others that my parents gave people money to win their affections. This impacted me deeply.

I realized that just as it's important to use wisdom with where I give my time and energy, it's just as important to use wisdom with where I give money.

*   *   *   *   *

I would rather have to learn to take better care of myself and to believe that I'm beautiful than to have to learn to be kind. I'm so grateful for her impact on my life in choosing kindness and generosity over fighting and selfishness.

I needed to find balance, though. It took years for me to learn to stand up for myself. I eagerly stood up for others. It was easy for me to overlook other people's mistakes and or wrong treatment of me, but I lost sleep when I believed someone else was upset with me. Thus, the allowance of others to run over me continued uninhibited.

*   *   *   *   *

In my late thirties, I made the decision to stand up for myself and to say no when needed. I proceeded to do so with much explanation as to why I might have to disappoint someone. A year later, I made the decision to say no without explaining why. Just say no and leave it at that.

There were people in my life who would tell me about a project they were doing because they knew I'd drop everything and go help them.

It was unfair to my husband because I'd turn myself inside out to help others to the point of exhaustion, which meant I'd had nothing left to give him at the end of the day. I neglected my own work to help others.

In quiet desperation, to convince myself that I was enough, I made myself invaluable to others. Surely this meant I was enough, but I came to a season where I felt sad when I was told I was the kindest person someone else knew. I wanted to be more than kind.

It started with me knowing I was completely loved by God without having to achieve or earn anything. I was then able to live with disappointing others and knew that the world wouldn't fall apart if someone was displeased with me. I gradually became able to just be me and discover that I actually had talents besides kindness.

I don't have to be liked. I still feel uncomfortable that someone may not like me, but that's okay. It's alright for me not to be everyone's cup of tea.

*   *   *   *   *

She builds others up because she knows what it's like to be torn down. ~ Anthem Lights

23

Credit or No Credit

She believed she could so she did.

What if I didn't need credit? There were numerous times throughout my life that I became upset when another person took credit for something I did.

I sought to help others in each season of my life. I suppose many times it was in helping others that I found self-worth. When someone took credit for what I did, the pat on my back was taken away too.

Growing up one of nine siblings, I was the quiet one whose voice was easily drowned out as we sat around the dinner table. As everyone chatted about the day's events, it made it easier to be the invisible one who blended in with the wallpaper.

In my reaction to life, I made it easy for others to take credit for what was mine. My stronger, younger sister was my hero growing up. She learned early on to speak for me when I found it increasingly difficult to speak to anyone I didn't know. I desired her effortless ability to share her thoughts because I found myself tripping over words in any given situation.

My younger self thought this was what I wanted, but all too soon, I found myself wanting to have a voice, be heard, and be validated for me, not just one of my parent's children.

I didn't think of a future outside of getting married and having children. I did nothing to develop skills other than cooking, gardening, and housekeeping. But with a large family living on a busy dairy farm, there wasn't time for creative cooking as much as simply meeting the daily needs of filling my family's bellies.

While at twelve years old, I contemplated writing a story about a girl named Darcy, inspired by a book I'd read that year. I dreamed of the adventures she'd take, but that idea faded as daily life demanded my attention and growing up to be an author as an Amish married woman didn't seem at all likely.

*   *   *   *   *

About ten years into my marriage, Ivan and I moved to another state for work. It was a strange sensation to live in a new place away from all that was familiar. For the first ten years of married life, I deferred everything related to entertaining guests and social events to Mom, since she has always been incredibly gifted with hospitality.

After we moved, I began to consider what I enjoyed and only then began to find out what I was capable of. I realized that I had lived in my mom's shadow all those years, just as I lived in my husband's shadow, deferring my dreams for his. Deferring what I wanted, for what he wanted.

I started hosting an annual cookout for our friends and family. For the first three years, I'd be so stressed by the time the day before the cookout arrived that I'd get a migraine or break down in tears. It may sound crazy that I continued to host these cookouts, but the truth is, I loved to have guests and serve them. It's one of the ways I enjoy loving people.

It was another learning experience, where although there were growing pains, I came to the place where there was no stress involved in hosting. This taught me that I could accomplish anything I set my mind to practice until I became adept at it.

* * * * *

The better I got at the skills I worked to perfect, the more confidence I gained, thus, the less I worried about what others thought of my abilities, and the less I needed credit for something I accomplished.

While I don't think it's right to take credit for what someone else has accomplished, if I don't need credit, does it really matter?

What's beautiful to me is that each time credit was taken from me, I'd feel hurt and wronged, but it worked a beautiful peace in my heart. If the job gets done and another person receives what they have need of, and I don't need others to know I helped, then it really doesn't matter how it got done or by whom.

When another person steals credit for something I've done, they must need validation more than I do. Even though one can't truly enjoy a job well done if they didn't do it, I don't have to be the one to show them that truth. I learned this by example, and so will they.

* * * * *

It is amazing what you can accomplish if you do not care who gets the credit. ~ Harry S. Truman

Credit or No Credit

24

A Place of Grace

Owning our story and loving ourselves through that process is the bravest thing that we'll ever do. ~ Brene Brown

Fear has stolen far too many precious days from me. From the mild fear of voicing my views about something, to intense, heart racing, mind-numbing, frozen in place, unable to move fear. It has been such a major part of my life that to have come to the place that I know I'm safe and protected in unsafe situations is one of the most treasured gifts I've received.

What brings me peace is knowing that I am hidden under His wings when I need to be there or that He stands right behind me when I need to stand strong and take back that which was stolen from me.

A few years ago, as I was seeking to take back my life, going from a place of victim to victor, I began to have dreams of stolen treasure being returned to me.

One night as I slept, I dreamed of a gray haired, soft spoken woman with a slightly bowed back. She knocked on my door and asked to look for treasure that had been buried in the floor of my house. I let her in, and as she began to look around. She asked me to look at the floor. Suddenly, I noticed that someone had attempted to look for treasure in this floor twice before because there were two distinct places where the floor boards had been cut into and nailed shut again. As she opened it for the third time, I immediately saw the treasure inside.

On another dream filled night, a woman of similar characteristics knocked on my door and handed me a handful of recipe cards that she confessed to have stolen from me years ago.

I realized that these dreams were types and shadows of what I was realizing in my waking hours. I was indeed taking back my life, my voice, my journey, making all the dark moments worth waiting through.

* * * * *

Many times, women are incredibly cruel to each other. Instead of supporting each other, we criticize and compete.

Many of the accusations that have played over and over in my head are statements I've heard made about others.

For instance, when a woman wears something new or different, how many times have we heard, "Who does she think she is?" or "I would never wear something like that!" We judge, hoping to receive validation at our core.

When we feel secure in who we are, we have no need to criticize. Instead, we bless the courage in others, even when it's different than what we'd choose.

Being loved for who we are is the most profound need of our hearts and is truly the sweetest gift.

Why then, do we seek to be like someone else? Perhaps we're convinced that they are smarter, prettier, and their life is more put together, or perhaps we believe we're unlovable, and if people really get to know us, they'd see our flaws and decide they don't like us after all.

* * * * *

For years, I withheld my love from people thinking I had to remain on the outside. I believed the lie that were someone to get too close, they'd see how flawed I was and criticize my weakness. I myself was the harshest of critic of me.

If you would've asked me if I loved others, I would have been quick to assure you I did, but I didn't realize how guarded I kept my heart.

To love others unconditionally, I had to love myself first. Each time I sought to love another wholeheartedly, the walls protecting me from pain blocked me from loving with abandon.

*   *   *   *   *

At the heart of every woman is the little girl in her that still wants to be liked and accepted. As we grow older, we begin to feel that it's okay if not everyone likes us, and although we still care what people think, it doesn't devastate us to find that we're not everyone's idea of the perfect girl. What we believe and or what's important to us outweighs another person's opinion of us.

We have allowed the snares of shame, defeat, fear, and guilt to turn us against each other instead of lifting each other up and providing a healing balm to those who've fallen by the way or to those who need an encouraging word.

I know that I do not need to compete with anyone. I am uniquely created to be me, and I'm confident in my identity. I'm reminded of one of my favorite quotes,

A flower doesn't think of competing with the flower next to it, it just blooms. ~ Anonymous

*   *   *   *   *

I struggled for years to overcome the pain of my mom not only failing to protect me, but also for punishing me for what was done to me. While today I clearly understand her intent and the fear that propelled her to react, I then saw it as betrayal from one woman to another.

The gift to me in Mom's response was that I understand that many times women are unprepared to deal with such a thing and feel helpless. Therefore, doing what women have always done, they hide, deny it ever happened, and sweep it under the carpet, making it go away.

For a time, it does go away, or at least it appears to, but it lurks in the secret corners of a woman's heart, for she sees through the glasses of shame, guilt, and fear.

It is my opinion, in part by experience, that she reacts to violation by either seeking to steer clear of men, becoming promiscuous, or in mildest form, simply driving all of it inward to the deepest recesses of her heart.

When she hides it away in her heart, it eats away at the very essence of her. Its stain taints the way she loves those closest to her, her family, husband, and or children. Although she seeks to give her whole heart, in protecting the secrets, a part of her heart remains hidden away, fearing that others will see inside.

These hidden secrets begin to lose the power of their shameful grip when we allow light inside. We find that to keep it hidden is more painful than to expose it to the light of day.

*   *   *   *   *

You gain strength, courage, and confidence by every experience in which you really stop to look fear in the face. You must do the thing which you think you cannot do. ~ Eleanor Roosevelt

Authenticity is the daily practice of letting go of who we think we're supposed to be and embracing who we are. ~ Brene Brown

A Place of Grace

Blessing My Body

Before you speak; think. Is it true? Is it helpful? Is it inspiring?
Is it necessary? Is it kind?

For all the days I spent cursing my body and despising myself for being weak and less than perfect, I will spend just as many days and more to bless my body.

Initially, the thought of baring my soul on paper for the world to see terrified me. The idea of opening my heart to the point of allowing anyone who wishes to judge and criticize the words from my heart was almost enough to silence the words forever, but alas, how can the butterfly remain in the cocoon forever? It can't, for it would die if the cocoon wouldn't burst first.

Blessing My Body

My heart sought to speak more than the enemy of my soul fought to convince me that the lies he spoke into my ears were truth. I felt compelled to use my voice more than I felt compelled to protect my thoughts from criticism. When my heart heard the quiet truth whispered, it recognized it as the voice of the author of my soul. The longer the truth was whispered, the quieter the accusations parading as truth became. I shall seek to be authentic all the days of my life.

*   *   *   *   *

A letter I wrote to myself...

Dear Kate,

For the times you were afraid, and I made fun of you for being weak, for the times you weren't strong enough to stand on your own, and I despised you, for all this time that you ate food to protect yourself from people and fear, and I shamed you for it, I'm sorry.

You are beautifully made. You are strong. You are my hero, and I believe in you. I love who you are, and you are more than enough. Thank you for always having my back even when I was not a friend to you. I'm thankful that you are strong enough to bend, but you won't break. You are resilient just like your mama. I'm thankful for you.

From the girl in the mirror

The most challenging thing for me to learn in life hasn't been to love others, but to love myself.

"The second is equally important: 'Love your neighbor as yourself.' No other commandment is greater than these."

~ **Mark 12:31 (NLT)**

*   *   *   *   *

What if whatever we focus on grows?

If this is true, do I want to give voice to the faults and flaws and harp on them, or do I want to draw attention to how much I'm loved and accepted?

I've found that the more I focus on how much I'm loved and how He sees me, the more freely I love others.

I don't fear the reaction of others when I'm at peace and know with every confidence that I'm secure in where I stand. I am different and this is what makes my voice unique. If I don't write my story, it'll never be told.

If I don't become the author of my life, it'll be a life of reaction instead of a life of response to the drawing and pulling of His voice within me that drowned out the false accusations appearing real, replacing them with calm assurance and quiet acceptance that merits no explanation.

The faults and flaws that glared in my face since my youth began to shrink and have grown fainter as my knowing I'm loved and accepted has grown.

*   *   *   *   *

"She is clothed with strength and dignity; she can laugh at the days to come." ~ Proverbs 31:25 (NIV)

26

A Place of Peace

Sometimes when you're in a dark place, you think you've been buried, but you've actually been planted. ~ Christine Caine

From a young age, both of my children have struggled with anxiety. It's been a revealing look in the mirror for me to see them experience much the same as I have. When I first realized it, I was devastated because I diligently sought to fill their hearts with positive affirmations to ensure that they didn't suffer as I did.

Many days of quiet desperation filled my life as I saw how miserably I failed as a mother. I loved them with every fiber of my being, and yet, my efforts just weren't enough.

Driving to town one day to get groceries, I stopped at a traffic light, once again overwhelmed with worry for my son, who was struggling in school. As I prayed, yet again, that God would keep him safe, help him, and show His love to him, I suddenly paused when my heart heard, "So you think you can protect him better than I?"

My heart melted. Faced with a "look in the mirror" moment, I saw myself with a white-knuckle grip concerning my children's well-being. The numerous times I shared with friends and family about my son's intense struggle with anxiety played through my mind.

I stopped.

I began to thank God that He has my child and that He will take care of the little piece of my heart walking on the outside of my body, just as He takes care of me.

*   *   *   *   *

The following week, my son's teacher asked me what happened

to my son? It was as though he was a different person.

That experience was a beautiful revelation to the position I have in my children's lives.

I was given the gift to be their mother, to protect them from harm in the ways that are in my control, to love and nurture them, and to see to their well-being, but I was not given the position of shielding them from the life experience that is uniquely theirs.

I had been giving voice to the anxiety by speaking of it often. As I began to speak peace over my son and simply thank God for His grace and blessing on my child, peace filled more of the spaces that anxiety ruled in before. The anxiety didn't disappear altogether, but it lessened.

What if, just as I was giving strength to the anxiety in my child's life, I was also keeping him from the life that is his to experience by my desperate attempts to protect him from pain?

What if what I give attention to grows?

Growing up, I gave my attention to fear, my being fat, my shame, and my protection of myself. In raising my children, I gave all my energy to loving them and protecting them from all conceivable pain. I reacted to fear and anxiety with anxiety and fear.

Peace grew as I responded to fear and anxiety with peace. Calm was amplified when peace was magnified.

* * * * *

How lovely the silence of growing things. ~ Anonymous

27

Broken Gifts

Peace is not absence of conflict, it is the ability to handle conflict by peaceful means. ~ Ronald Reagan

The safest place in my childhood was when Mom would read to us. After the day's work of cooking, doing laundry with the wringer washer with the small but loud motor that powered the washer, cleaning, milking our small herd of dairy cows, and the dinner dishes were put away, we'd pile around her as she begged us not to sit on her.

The story came alive under the spell of her words. Without electricity, there was no entertainment except that which we created in our minds. Mom painted a vivid picture with each chapter she read. Story time always ended with a chorus of, "One more chapter mom, please?"

After story time, Dad would tuck us in and wait for us to say our bedtime prayers. The patience he showed while listening to us thank God for the curtains, the barn to keep the animals safe, the oil lamps that lit our evenings after night had fallen, and any other random detail that would pop into our minds was amazing. I really couldn't blame him if he'd admit today that he fell asleep a time or two.

*   *   *   *   *

My parents poured love into me as they raised me with all the capacity they had and sought God in all they did, and despite having struggled through many painful moments in their own childhoods, by example, they instilled within me the resilience we are gifted with as human beings. They were the perfect parents to create the environment for me to seek my purpose in life and to become who I am today. They are proud of me, and I'm ever so blessed to call them my people.

*   *   *   *   *

What if it doesn't matter where we come from or what our lineage is, and we became who we are in response to the gifts and talents that we're given and what we do with them, seeking to live authentic and not trying to be like someone else?

What matters to me is that I fulfill the life that is mine to live, not giving space for comparing myself to another who naturally exhibits the areas I'm lacking in.

As I seek to see who I am with gratitude and be true to who that is, the desire to be as another dwindles. Instead, anticipation over the prospect of that which I've yet to discover about this girl who I fought so long and hard to avoid, fills my days with barely contained excitement.

The profound gratitude that fills my heart to overflowing when I think of this life I was gifted to live uniquely me, brings incredible joy. As dark as my darkest moments were, the opposite is pure, unrequited joy for the journey set before me, for that which is to be.

*   *   *   *   *

For the times I've been alone or thought I was, I'm grateful. For the moments I asked God where He was and why He didn't keep me from pain, I'm grateful. In looking back over my life, I see the ways that He was in the dark places with me. I just didn't see Him as He was. I wanted to see Him from my point of view and not from the way He entrusted me with the dark places.

Having visited the desolate places and knowing from the deepest place of my being that in restoration, the darkest places will become the platform whereby I will bring hope and peace to others. After having been there, my heart recognizes the dark places in others and in recognition replaces light with dark.

What if the darkest place you've ever been is to be redeemed to become your gift? It's okay if this question makes you feel angry. What a grandiose suggestion, right?

What if in having been in your darkest place, you became every person? You know the hardest place, you've felt every shameful, guilty thought and heart pain that has ever existed? You know what it is to wear shame as your ever-faithful coat which shields you from the cold?

What purpose could it possibly serve but to destroy you?

Could it be that you were given this to know the deepest despair and heart crushing pain of another, and in your healing, you place light where desolation was the only thing known until they feel the kindred emotions and hope in your eyes that give way to the hope of rescue from the deep abiding, bitter cup they've drank from since their youth?

You were there. You know what hides behind the curtain so carefully constructed to paint the proper picture for the world to see. In having been there, you see through the curtain that can only be seen by one who knows.

*   *   *   *   *

If it costs you your peace, it's too expensive. ~ Anonymous

Broken Gifts

28

Beautifully Imperfect

There is nothing more rare, nor more beautiful than a woman being unapologetically herself; comfortable in her perfect imperfection. To me, that is the true essence of beauty. ~ Steve Maraboli

Today I realize that my parents were the perfect people to give birth to me and love me to adulthood. It wasn't their responsibility to do everything right. It was their responsibility to love me and protect me to the best of their ability, and they did that.

I receive the gift of their love and lifetime investment in my well-being with a grateful heart. As an adult, it is now entirely up to me what happens to the rest of my life. It's up to me to choose to do well with or squander the dedication they poured into growing me up.

Will I reward them with a life well lived or spend it being bitter over the things that hurt me? I choose grace, and I choose to live well.

*   *   *   *   *

What if the people who hurt me weren't the source, but simply the avenue whereby to destroy me?

If not by an impressionable person, many words and or hurtful acts wouldn't carry much weight.

We get to choose our friends, but we don't get to choose our family or guardians. Thus, it makes every bit of sense that it's exactly why the most harmful things we experience throughout our childhood are by those closest to us, therefore having the greatest impact. If a stranger hurts us, we can avoid further contact with them, and the negative impact ceases. But if we are hurt by a trusted guardian, the ability to harm remains. It is only by growing and by it being revealed to us that the negative impact loses its hold over us.

Many of the lies I believed about myself from childhood only lost their hold when I recognized the truth of who I really am.

Had I known to the degree that I do today how much I'm loved by my creator, my life up to this point would've been a life of grace, rest, and peace, but the gift in that I didn't know may be that I wouldn't have appreciated it as much as I do today.

For all the days of torment I lived in by believing the lies about myself, I shall spend that many days and more in resting and being grateful that He has redeemed the time, and each hard thing became a strength in my life.

In resting that He has made all things perfect in His time, that which sought to destroy me loses its power, and I'm left with profound gratitude for the life lessons the attempted destroyer has provided me.

The people in my life, who at one point caused me pain, were my gift. Recognizing their words or deeds as lies, stripped the lies of their power over me.

*   *   *   *   *

The painful things we've experienced often leave a hole in our hearts. When a dad, mom, husband, or wife chooses to leave because their capacity to give stopped where their guilt began, and they stay out of your life because it hurts too much to stay, you are enough.

Their ability to give or lack thereof has nothing to do with who you are. Their demons scream louder than their capacity to give. The hole in their heart is bigger than their love for you.

Allow His love to fill your heart. Know that through His healing, love, and forgiveness, you have the grace to heal from what your parent or spouse couldn't give you. Know that healing and wholeness in your heart can do for your parent what they wish they could have done for you.

You are loved just as you are, and you are given grace and healing to finish what those before you began but were unable to finish. The bounty of grace is yours to receive. Regardless of the size of the hole in your heart, it is small enough to be filled with His love and heal those around you with endless grace and peace.

What if in healing the hurts uniquely yours, your purpose is revealed, and you in turn heal those you meet?

*　*　*　*　*

Who better understands what the one who lost their child far too soon feels like better than the one who has walked that same path?

Who better understands the demons of one who struggles with alcohol or drugs to escape their pain than the one who has recovered from this way of coping?

Who better feels for the one who carries more weight than is needed than the one who has carried it themselves?

The common bond of empathy covers all pain, but there's something beautiful about two hearts connecting in a mutual experience that words find difficult to express.

Where words fail, an expression of love does beautifully.

What if the scars tell a story of hope, redemption, and grace? What if in replacing the bitterness with all-encompassing love, the oil of pure love flows from His heart to yours, and He reveals to you the same beauty within your heart that I've found in mine?

What would it be to see wholeness where there was brokenness? Gold filled cracks healing the wounds of the heart now stronger than had it never been wounded.

*   *   *   *   *

For many of the early years of my life, I struggled with self-consciousness to the point that many times I would've preferred avoiding social events, but I made myself go even when it meant blushing often and stumbling verbally through the day each time.

When I became aware of the fact that self-consciousness is a form of pride, I sought hard to overcome this fault. In preparing for an event, my mantra became this, "Kate, get over yourself, this is not about you. Go make it about them."

The more confident I became in who I am, and the more I quit worrying about what people thought of me, the better I became in social situations. Today, I have little problem initiating conversation with anyone. I never imagined that the day would come when I wouldn't meet a stranger.

What's interesting to me is that growing up, when someone didn't talk to me, my first thought was, "What is wrong with me, or what did I do?"

Today I realize that most of the time, when another person seems standoffish, it seldom has anything to do with me. Most of the time, if I start a conversation, that person warms up and relaxes.

There's no difference between you and the celebrity you seek to be like. You are just as important. Both of you put your coat on one arm at a time.

*   *   *   *   *

I start many things and don't finish them. I have many brilliant ideas, but I don't see them through. I seek perfection in housekeeping, but I get overwhelmed when I pull everything out of every closet I have and then clutter every surface of my little house until it drives me to tears. When I still lived at home, there were seven girls to assist with the weekly house cleaning, but I imagine that by my efforts alone, I'll be able to do all my deep cleaning in one day.

For years, I condemned myself for doing life imperfectly, forgetting that it takes little to do for many what it takes much to do for one.

My ability to love is imperfect, but my capacity to love is vast.

I'm infinitely grateful for the life I've been given and for the season I get to live in. Even though the world is colder today than it's ever been, His presence and love is more tangible than it's ever been. I'm truly blessed that I was given the gift of my family and the gift of living today, right now, right here.

*   *   *   *   *

Alive. Blessed. Grateful.

29

Lies Appearing True

Start each day with a grateful heart.

How different my life would've been in my youth had I known to see myself through God's eyes, but if I would've known that, no doubt my struggles would've looked different, but no less painful.

We view life through the lenses of our experiences. Often, the things that happen to us aren't as difficult as the mind games that result from those experiences.

For me, the sexual molestation wasn't nearly as bad as it is for many children, but that didn't keep the enemy of my soul from sinking burning arrows of shame, guilt, and fault where he knew it'd sink fast and hard.

As children, we accept the blame for each situation we find ourselves in. Innocence exists at each turn, but little by little, as mental, physical, and spiritual violation occurs, innocence is lost and shame and guilt grows as our young impressionable minds remain trapped by our inability to express our thoughts.

*   *   *   *   *

For years, my son has talked about an evening we all decided to go see a movie. He insisted that he woke up in his car seat after a nap to discover that the rest of us had gone into the theater and watched the movie without him. I did my best to convince him that I would never leave him alone in the car. I explained to him that as much of a worry wart as I was, I couldn't have relaxed if I had left him in the car, but no amount of persuasion alleviated him of that perception.

My son, as a little boy, learned to defend his honor by making a lot of noise if he felt threatened or angry with his big sister. It didn't take long for this mama to look for the noise behind the noise. Frequently, he and his sister would fight, and it took discreet observation to figure out who was in the wrong.

Many times, it proved to be that the quiet one was the instigator, but on a few different occasions, my son was reprimanded after a sudden loud howl. Today he believes that we picked on him because we loved his big sister more. Despite my efforts to assure him that I saw past the yelling and that I loved him just as much as his sister, he remains convinced of his view of the situation. That view may never change.

Different instances over the years, as the ones I just mentioned, helped me to understand that the enemy of our soul sometimes uses children's perception to help reinforce their personal belief that they are not people of value.

I know I would never have left my son in the car for any event or loved his sister more than him, but because he viewed it that way, it made him think he wasn't loved as much as his sister and no amount of reasoning convinced him differently.

Many times, as an adult, by going over an event of impact from my childhood in my mind, I realized that the intent of the person who hurt me was often innocent.

I accepted lies as truth because of my young mind's perception and how it made me feel.

Today, as an adult, those memories and perceptions lose their power over me because I get to view them from an adult perspective, and with each revelation, peace replaces pain and misunderstanding.

*   *   *   *   *

If you must look back, do so forgivingly. If you must look forward, do so prayerfully. However, the wisest thing you can do is be present in the present...Gratefully. ~ Maya Angelou

30

Authentically Me

Find the courage to be authentic, not everyone will like you, but no one can if they don't get a chance to know you. ~ Lori Deschene

This past summer, I attended my grade school reunion. I walked on the gravel lined driveway of the one room with a partition in the middle, parochial schoolhouse, convinced that the driveway had shortened in length since I was there a few short years ago.

Entering the building through the basement door, the dank odor of earth, cement, and aged wood assailed my nostrils. A long shelf lined the basement wall where lunch boxes of various forms, shapes, and sizes await noon lunch hour when school is in session. Curved black coat hooks were placed immediately beneath the shelf. I imagined the bendy, black, rubber boots on the floor. Off to my right, the lonely little sink of running water, albeit cold only, stood with a much-used-bar of blue soap.

Upstairs, I entered the room, taking in the chalkboard with hints of cloudy white streaks and smudges, remembering the smell of new crayons and crisp, clean, white paper so vivid I imagined it was real. I recalled how relieved I felt when Teacher decided to punish the boys if they scratched the board with their nails provoking goose bumps to stand at attention. An old clock stood front and center, ticking loudly in the stillness. Faithful letters of the alphabet still lined the wall near the ceiling.

This room held some sweet and pensive memories, such as when a classmate tripped another student as he walked by, causing restrained giggles to ripple through the room, eliciting a stern response from Teacher.

I was lucky to attend a small school where everyone knew each other, and aside from an occasional squabble, we were a close-knit group.

Ever seeking to blend in, I was ashamed when a classmate remarked at the funny way I sneezed. The next time I sneezed, I tried to keep it quiet and change the sound of it.

On another occasion, one of the boys commented on my weird way of running on the playground at recess, prompting me to try to run in a more composed manner.

Despite all my insecurities, I loved school and never wanted to graduate or at least that's what I thought in eighth grade. I may have changed my mind, had I had the opportunity to go on to high school.

My perception has come full circle. Where as a child I sought desperately to fit in and not cause any ripples, after visiting one of the memorable places of my childhood as an adult, I realize that each child struggles to find their way in life.

Through the eyes of an adult, there is peace in my heart toward the younger me and I salute her for her resilience.

*   *   *   *   *

I'm profoundly grateful for the love that is God.

By growing up in religion, I learned all the ways that religion perceived God kept one in line by holding the promise of fire and brimstone over my head. It evoked the desire in me to walk a very straight line.

How sweet is it, then, to discover His unconditional love for me?

Instead of trying desperately to conduct my life perfectly, I received the beautiful gift of realizing that I can't do it all perfectly, and that it's okay. I'm entirely and completely loved regardless of my performance.

*   *   *   *   *

The truth is uncomfortable to discuss, that is, unless one decides that nothing is worth hiding. ~ Kate Troyer

About the Author

 Kate Troyer is a writer, speaker, and a dedicated advocate for women in finding their voice, finding healing and restoration for the wounds of childhood, and overcoming the limits they believe the experiences from childhood created for them. Kate's mission in life is to share with and inspire women to discover their voice and experience the beauty of living a life of emotional wellness which leads to a life of wholeness. Kate shares her life with her husband, two kids, a menagerie of animals on a small ever-expanding little farm in Northeast, Ohio.

Contact Information

Find Kate on Facebook, Pinterest, Twitter, and Instagram: @ KateTroyer

Email Kate @: ktroyer13@gmail.com